Gorman on

California Premium Wines

Robert Gorman

Gorman on California Premium Wines
is published by
Ten Speed Press
Post Office Box 4310
Berkeley, California 94704

Cover design and photography by
Brenton Beck
Drawing, page 219, by
Anne Koenig

Production by Fifth Street Design Associates

The publisher wishes to thank Marge Malone and John Piane
for their efforts in the preparation of the manuscript
for this book.

ISBN 0–913668–50–8 pb: ISBN 0–913668–51–6 cloth
Printed in the United States of America

For Norman and Kleo Mini

Table of Contents

vi Contents

Part One

Introduction

During the first half of this century Americans passed through a curiously awkward phase of national culture. The sources of aesthetic enjoyment were more or less limited to the motion picture, the newspaper, the magazine and the automobile. Eating and drinking were assigned to the lowest of necessary functions. With a kind of stoic determination, we told ourselves that food was little more than fuel necessary to keep the human engine going in a hyper-industrialized world. Anything beyond a statement of reverence for "Mom's Apple Pie" was looked upon with suspicion. Interest in food and wine was considered enervating and demoralizing.

Perhaps only within the last fifteen or twenty years, our new affluence, leisure, and love of travel have served to broaden the horizon of our aesthetic enjoyments. Along with a new interest in the fine arts, we have developed a taste for excellence in food and particularly in wine. Many of us have revolted from a surfeit of over-processed, plasticized, impersonal food. We have discovered that fine food and wine are sources of quite extraordinary enjoyment—enjoyment which demands more than just passing notice. We have come to understand that the quality of our enjoyments, far from being enervating, spurs and supports the quality of work. This country has been undergoing a general humanizing process. Our experience with fine food and wine has inspired enthusiasm, discrimination and a lively inquiry into the ways that excellence is achieved. We are at the point where we can share the conviction of most civilized people that food and wine are worthy of a considerable amount of attention: that they are objects of aesthetic perception.

While there are varying degrees of art involved in the preparation of food, wine is most assuredly an artistic creation. Wine is not a "natural" object. As Professor Amerine has reminded us, "If 'God' had his 'natural way', vinegar, not wine, would be the result. Wine is surely man-made if it is to be good or fine. Every minutiae of planting, growing the vines, of harvesting, fermenting and processing must be followed if the finest wine is to be produced. There is no doubt that good wine is one of man's finest artistic creations."[1]

By saying that wine is a work of art, this is not meant to imply that wine has "meaning". A wine does not have to "mean" anything to be a work of art any more than a painting has to represent something in order to be a work of art. Perhaps the deadliest bore of all is the person who takes wine so seriously as to make it an end in itself, a source of "meaning". I cannot help but think of Richard Benjamin's devastating portrait of the wine-snob husband in the film "Diary of a Mad Housewife"! As in everything else, it is a matter of keeping the proper perspective. The *raison d'etre* of a fine wine is to grace a table at which civilized people gather to enjoy fine cuisine and the pleasure of each other's company. The marvelous Cabernet that you are serving to your guests might indeed be made from grapes picked at the *south* end of the vineyard, but let this be implicit in the sparkling eyes of your guests, making marvelous and witty conversation with you at your dinner table. Great food and wine is an achievement of great balance and harmony; that it serves to inspire well-being, enjoyment, the harmony of friendships and the warmth of family bonds, makes it certainly one of the highest forms of civilization.

We are experiencing an emergent connoisseurship of wine in this country along with a new sense of artistry in the making of wine, and yet so little of our native literature reflects this renaissance. Much of the writing seems to be based on press releases (i.e., what the winemakers would like us to think of themselves) rather than a hard-nosed look at the wine. It has taken three Englishmen—Harry Waugh, Hugh Johnson and Kathleen Bourke—to write on California wine with any depth and sense of perspective; and we have had a very fresh, direct look at a broad range of California wines in the buyers' guide of Hurst Hannum and Robert Blumberg, *The Fine Wines of California*.

---

[1] San Francisco Magazine, October, 1972, p. 56.

My book is not a buyers' guide. It is the record of a personal voyage of discovery into the premium wines of California, and a distillation of some of the reflections I have made on them and conversations I have had about them.

I have no professional connection with the wine business, but I make no apologies for my lack of professional status. If my book has a bias, it is biased toward the consumer, the emergent connoiseur who, like myself, is in the process of educating his palate and building a wine cellar.

"Personal" does not mean subjective or arbitrary. There is no ultimate court which sits to judge the merits of wines, providing us poor "subjective" wine lovers with some "objective" hierarchy of fine wines. Granted, there is a vague consensus which develops, based on the opinions of professional people who have tasted a great deal of wine. This consensus can be useful, but ultimately, the wines should give *us* pleasure, should appeal to *our* sense of good taste. After all, we, the consumers, are footing the bill for the entire enterprise of growing grapes and making, packaging and distributing wine.

I was sampling wine in the tasting room of a prestigious winery not too long ago and commented to the host that, with all due respect for the quality of the wines, I personally preferred comparable but considerably less costly wines of other winemakers. The rather indignant reply was that several "experts" had rated their wines among the finest made in California and that these high ratings warranted the higher prices. And furthermore, that my own subjective predilections counted for very little. I am not sure whether this was the official attitude of the house or whether the host was merely an over-zealous, self-ordained prophet of his revered employer. Is there anyone in his right mind who would fail to take offense at such nonsense?

Of course, there will always be those people (especially Americans) who demand, at whatever the cost, what the "experts" consider the best, not so much for their immediate use and enjoyment, but for the supposed status which owning them is thought to confer. What an expensive and empty satisfaction!

Independent judgment and personal good taste count for a great deal in choosing and enjoying wine, or any product, for that matter. Unfortunately, there are not many Americans who take the trouble to develop independent, reflective judgment and make careful comparisons. So many people cannot buy anything unless they are *sold* on it. When all the sales pitches, all the publicity, all the hard-sell commercials, all the fads and styles have passed, there are a few basic criteria which remain to guide most sensible people in judging the value of anything purchased for personal enjoyment. Is it well crafted? Does one take pleasure in the way it was put together? Does it come together with style and beauty? Does it fulfill its function well? Does it give pleasure?

I have devoted a fair portion of this book to reflections on how fine wine is put together, with a view to understanding the options which a creative winemaker takes to breed quality and style into his wine.

In the early nineteen twenties, Gertrude Stein told Americans to take a much closer, more careful look at things which are crafted for our pleasure. She taught that fine works of art not only hold up under close scrutiny, but reveal unsuspected riches. In the case of paintings, she urged us to look and look and look again, and to look at all kinds of paintings, old ones, new ones, great ones, and poor ones. Not at the "picture" so much as the way that the artist applied paint to the canvas to build up a representation. Her advice might well be applied to the way one approaches wine as an aesthetic object.

The choice of a wine or any aesthetic object, involves a certain amount of personal creativity and self-expression. It is not so much a matter of impressing one's friends as it is expressing oneself to them, through good taste and style, and sharing one's enjoyments with them. There is not only an art to choosing wine but an art to balancing fine food with appropriate wines. I have given some attention in this book to the art of serving wine and hope that my reflections will be helpful.

And since making a fine wine does not go on in a vacuum, but is inevitably a business, I have given some attention to the economics of the wine business in California.

I wish to thank Darrell Corti, Norman Mini, and John Piane who read parts of the manuscript and offered valuable suggestions and encouragement. Several Bay Area wine merchants and their staffs have been immensely helpful. So many of these fine merchants have very generously shared their time, their knowledge and their vast experience with me—not as a writer about wines (only one was aware that I was writing a book)—but simply as an interested and reasonably articulate consumer. I should, however, thank Ken Kew and his staff at Esquin's for some special favors.

Premium Winemaking in California
and the New American
Connoisseurship of Wine

One

To understand the present state of fine winemaking in California and wine connoisseurship in this country, a little history is in order.

We do not really have a well documented history of winemaking in California from the introduction of the vine in 1824 up until Prohibition. Though there is a great deal of background information and wine lore, there are virtually no careful descriptions of how the wines tasted. We do know that tremendous quantities of poor to very good beverage wine was made in California during this period and that a small minority of winemakers struggled to maintain a tradition of fine winemaking. Nob Hill grandees, fattened on gold-rush and railroad profits, stocked their cellars with these well made wines. Among the winemakers were Gustave Niebaum of Inglenook, James Wetmore at Cresta Blanca, Joseph Schram, Charles Krug, Paul Masson, and others. The celebrated Schramsburger Hock of Joseph Schram found its way onto the wine lists of fashionable London clubs, and Wetmore's Cresta Blanca wines won prizes at the Paris Exposition of 1900. The antique Inglenook wines which surfaced recently at the Heublein Auction attest to the quality of these Victorian wines.

By the turn of the century, San Francisco had become a wine-mad town. A great many wine loving Europeans were settling in California while thousands of young Californians, sons of the 49'ers, had gone off to Europe to learn the arts, sample *la vie boheme*, and discover the pleasure of wine. On their return most of them joined San Francisco's notorious Bohemian Club. Artists and winemakers rubbed elbows at the Club—the Wentes, the Wetmores and others. One of the artist members, Charles Rollo Peters, was selling his paintings for as much as $1000, and a good portion of this money was spent on huge vinous dinner parties which he threw regularly at his Monterey Hacienda. This was also the period during which many of San Francisco's restaurants and hotel dining rooms achieved gastronomic greatness.

But there were great setbacks: severe frosts, periods of glut which brought the price of wine down to eleven cents a gallon, the phylloxera devastation of the late eighteen-eighties, and, at the peak of wine production in California, the most devastating of all: Prohibition. Winemaking in California was reduced to the production of sacramental wines and to home winemaking. Most rootstocks were grafted over to thick-skinned, low quality grape varieties which were suitable for shipping to home winemakers throughout the country.

Immediately following Prohibition, the cocktail, not wine, became the All-American drink. Liquor was very inexpensive. A pint of rye whiskey could be bought for $1.25, but the poor quality needed a bit a camouflage—the Bronx, the Side-Car, the Stinger and other mixed drinks became part of the new ritual of the cocktail, one of the cornerstones of life in a racy, jazzy, "Art Deco" America.

The wine industry, crippled from Prohibition, embarked on a concentrated program of recovery. Their aim was to produce good quality beverage wines and to develop a wide ranging program to merchandise these wines to the American consumer. The Wine Institute was organized in 1934 to speak for the industry and help educate the American public about wine.

As a function of the necessity to create a new market, wine producers developed the "full-product line"—a whole galaxy of wines to suit every taste under a single brand name: Burgundy, Claret, Hock, Chablis (a supposedly drier white), Sauterne(s) (supposedly off-dry), Haut Sauterne(s) (noticeably sweet), Champagne, Port, Tokay, etc., etc.[1] Producers encouraged the consumer to buy on the basis of brand loyalty. Americans had been conditioned to make buying judgments on that basis so that its extension to wine was not difficult.

---

[1] Wines named and modeled after European prototypes (Hock, Claret, Burgundy, etc.) have come to be known in California as *generic* wines.

The emergence of the product line system was not entirely a matter of organized intent. Each winery was looking at all the others to see what their next move would be. If a winery came out with a Haut Sauterne(s), then several others would follow suit.

In practice, the product line proved to be a success because it gained shelf space in the stores for the products of the winery. The broader the product line, the more space allotted to the line, and the more attention was drawn to the brand.

There were certain other advantages to the full product line. The diversity of production utilized winery equipment and personnel over a much longer period of time. Each wine acted as a hedge against the others. There was no major disaster if one or two of the wines turned out badly. The wineries did not have "all their eggs in one basket".

Because of the start-up investment necessary to buy winemaking equipment and develop a system of merchandising, the function of growing grapes was left almost entirely in the hands of the farmer (or rancher as he is more commonly known in California). Most winemakers had little control over what went on in the vineyards. Grapes were sold on the free market and the free market dictated the price which was paid the grower for his grapes. Naturally, this system discouraged the planting of premium quality, low yielding grape varieties. As late as 1952, 88% of red wine grape acerage (including premium vineyard locations) was planted with the highest yielding varieties; namely, Alicante-Bouschet, Carignane and Zinfandel.

The system of distributing California wines had a profound effect, particularly in encouraging the branded product line system. In the years before prohibition, most wine made in California was shipped in cask, either by ship to the east coast or by rail or barge to closer destinations. Although there was some estate bottling (Inglenook wines were always bottled at the winery), merchants sold most of their wine out of cask or did some of their own bottling. By the 1930's the trucking industry had changed all that. After prohibition most wines were bottled at the winery and sold to distributors. The wineries could not themselves assume the responsibility and costs of distribution; and the function of wine distribution, unable to pay its own way, became grafted onto the system of distributing distilled spirits.

As had always been the case in California, there were a few winemakers who dedicated themselves to making wines of special quality. In the period following Prohibition, some exceptionally fine wines were made by Kurt Opper at Fountaingrove (Sonoma County). Inglenook Cabernet Sauvignon maintained its reputation as the finest red wine made in California. A small lot of very fine post-Prohibition Cabernet from the old Simi Winery (Healdsburg, Sonoma County) has come on the market recently, giving us some idea of the finer wines of the 1930's. Herman Wente was the giant in the area of white wine. His Livermore Valley Sauvignon Blanc was the classic white wine of this period. Other wineries were beginning to show interest in *varietal* bottlings—wines made from a single dominant grape variety and named after the variety. In 1936, Beaulieu, as well as Inglenook, was producing a Cabernet Sauvignon, and by 1940, Beaulieu, Louis Martini, Beringer and Larkmead had made varietals an important aspect of the line. This was not an entirely new practice in California as Victorian wine lists show a mix of varietal wines and generic wines.

World War II was something of a disaster for the making of fine wines in California. War-time economics had a profoundly adverse effect and the economic policies of the Roosevelt Administration were inimical to the wine industry. The shortage of alcohol brought the liquor industry closer still, solidifying its role as wine distributor, and creating an influence which has persisted ever since.

In spite of the convenience of this "marriage" between the wine industry and the distilled spirits industry, the relationship has had its unfortunate side effects. It fostered a tendency to think of wine in terms of distilled spirits—i.e., a perfectly clean, clear and completed product, invariable from year to year, ready for immediate consumption, and shelved and treated in the same manner as spirits. Bottle shops and restaurants "featured" a branded product line rather than make discriminating selections based on the merits of individual wines. Restaurants were themselves unsure about wine so they generally left the choice up to the distributor who obliged by making the selection and printing the wine list. In a situation like this, quality and appropriateness were not taken very seriously. The distributors were obviously most interested in selling the wines with the highest profit margins. This is why, even today, so many wine lists limit one's choice to the two least interesting lines of wines made in California: Paul Masson and Almaden. It is also the reason why one is confronted with wine lists in Chinese restaurants which recommend that you choose the red wine to go with your steaks and chops. Try to find the steaks and chops on the menu!

The war did not have totally adverse effects on the California wine industry. A great many Americans who went to war in Europe acquired a taste for wine while they were there and wine began to have some "grass-roots" appeal to Americans. At the same time, those few knowledgeable wine lovers who already existed in this country during and shortly after the war, were frustrated by greatly diminished supplies of European wine, and began to seek out quality domestic wines.

The recovery was painfully slow but progress was made; and by the 1950's the wineries began to prosper. In the early 1950's, wineries developed the institution known as the "tasting room". Prior to that time, those wineries who had wholesale distributors were prevented by law from having tasting facilities and retail shops.

Wineries were making and selling good wine and the system was working; but they tended to be complacent and parochial. Competition from European wines was not significant enough to force wineries to take a serious look at their potential competitors.

But there were major exceptions. Under the leadership and foresight of Drs. Amerine, Winkler, Olmo and others at the University of California at Davis, a brain-trust of oenologists was being built which would help in the coming effort to raise the overall quality of wine in California.

Quietly, unheralded, Andre Tchelistcheff, working within the product line system at Beaulieu, was making Cabernet Sauvignon, Pinot Noir and Chardonnay of remarkable quality, on a level with fine French wines. The Mondavis at Krug Winery, working within the product line system, produced a series of extraordinary Cabernets; and there were some fine Cabernets being made at Louis Martini as well. Starting in 1943, Lee Stewart almost single-handedly built Souverain Cellars, and in 1961 he produced a Cabernet Sauvignon which Harry Waugh judged to be on a level with his own Chateau Latour 1961.

John Daniel at Inglenook, Louis Martini, and, in the Livermore Valley, Herman Wente of Wente Brothers were making a special effort to lift the overall quality of California wines. By the early 1960's there was less tendency to parrot European place names. The trend was to let the wines appear under their own appellations—the place where they were grown and the variety of grape from which they were made.

Other somewhat heroic figures came on the scene, just after the war, building small estate wineries devoted to producing the finest quality wines possible. There were Jack and Mary Taylor who built up the small estate winery of Mayacamas, Fred McCrea of Stony Hill, Frank Bartholomew at Buena Vista, and most of all, the indomitable Martin Ray in Saratoga.

Following his retirement in 1948 as ambassador to Italy, J. D. Zellerbach, in conjunction with the very inventive winemaker, Brad Webb, founded Hanzell Winery in Sonoma, devoted entirely to the production of two fine wines, Chardonnay and Pinot Noir. Not much later, Joe Heitz came on the scene, setting a new pace and a new standard of excellence.

The early sixties introduced another very significant factor both for the development of fine wine in California and for the education of the American palate. America, unencumbered by the physical ravages of a World War, was much further along in achieving postwar prosperity than its European neighbors. It became a logical new market for the finer, more costly European wines. Three poor years in succession, 1956–57–58, made the situation all the more urgent, and a concentrated effort was made to introduce European wines to the American public. Nineteen fifty-nine was, fortunately, a year for wines with immediate and universal appeal, closely followed by "the year of the century", 1961. As a succession of fine vintages appeared, these wines conquered America. During the past decade and a half, the American palate has undergone a major revolution.

By the early 1960's, those winemakers who had laid an early foundation for premium wines were producing very high quality wines and were not only asking appropriately higher prices for them but were getting those prices. Both the success of these pioneers and the new interest in premium European wines had a profound effect. Within a decade, the California wine scene has virtually been turned upside-down. From the complacent mood of the 1950's, today the California wine industry is a scene of round-the-clock hard work and dedication, a tremendous spirit of renaissance. There has emerged a new generation of winemakers who are dedicating themselves to the goal of producing great premium wines, and I will take up their story in a later chapter.

A great deal of corporate capital has been pumped into the California wine scene in the past few years. The wine boom convinced several corporations that wine was a good, long-term investment. Some of the backing and encouragement went beyond the profit motive, approaching something akin to art patronage.

All the excitement, optimism, hard work and investment, is being borne out in the steady improvement in the quality of the wines. Within the past decade, California has shown signs that it might soon become one of the greatest viticultural areas of the world. Unfortunately, there is still a major stumbling block to progress—most Americans are reluctant to enjoy wine as a regular part of their diets.

Like all periods of hectic change, the transition has not gone on without its share of problems. In the same way that domestic wines became grafted onto the system of distributing distilled spirits, so too had much of the imported wines. These importer-distributors capitalized on a fundamental weakness of the majority of American consumers, and the American habit of buying on the basis of advertised brand names was misapplied to European Chateaux and Domaine bottlings. Considerations of the quality of individual vintages went, more or less, by the boards. The retailer, in most cases the liquor shop, had virtually no informed advice to offer the consumer. Many consumers bought indiscriminately and this sent the importers, with substantial capital reserves, back to Europe to buy the famous Chateaux wines ad libitum. The spiral continued. An over-heated market became bedazzled by the names of famous Chateaux. For many they became status objects which thay could flaunt in front of their peers. Speculators took further advantage of the situation and entered the market in 1970, driving the prices to absurd levels. Wine became a good investment for "smart money". But as price resistance mounted, clogging the pipe-lines of distribution, the market broke. The smart money johnny-come-latelies were left holding the bag. At least one wine investment organization went bankrupt.

In all fairness to the American wine buying public, it should be emphasized that during recent years a good many Americans have discovered the principle of cellar aging. A great many new American wine cellars have been built up from scratch in the past few years, stimulating tremendous additional demand.

Some of the distortions in the wine market have settled down recently and a great deal of the speculation has been shaken out of the system. Hopefully, we are entering a more sane market.

Wine fever in this country has generated a new business institution in the American market place—the wine merchant. This has been a mixed blessing. Some merchants have been an outpost of sanity through all the recent speculative madness, making selections which represent value for money and providing guidance which the American wine buyer needs so badly. Other wine merchants have preyed upon the susceptibility of the consumer for the snob appeal of wine and have taken every opportunity to price the wines as high as the traffic will bear.

The lover of fine wine in this country has reached a crucial point. If the drinking of fine wine is to be maintained as an integral part of civilized life and not just a luxury available to the very rich, it is up to the American wine lover to develop some degree of independence of judgment. With so many factors unrelated to intrinsic quality at work tending to inflate the price of fine wine, it is up to the American wine lover to take a hard-nosed, reflective, well-informed, independent attitude.

The technique of tasting and evaluating wine should be mastered. All too often it is assumed that the price tag immediately and accurately reflects intrinsic quality. All too often extraneous factors are at work in setting the asking price: heavy merchandising costs, speculative fever, sudden popularity, supply-demand, and a winemaker's over-blown opinion of himself. Truly fine wines are necessarily costly to make and will never be cheap, except by accident. *What is needed is judgment which recognizes value-for-money.* The American wine consumer should learn to shop more carefully. A little digging of one's own can turn up some exceptional values. The consumer should know where to go for the guidance of an experienced and reputable merchant, one who is steeped in the culture of wine and is dedicated to seeking out special quality and value for his customers.

Quality in wine is not just a happy accident, nor is it something which is "naturally" inherent in the wine itself. There is no simple definition of quality in wine. However, this much can be said: quality is founded upon two necessary and interrelated conditions—the skill and integrity of the producer and the discrimination of the consumer, his ability to recognize value and his willingness to say no when the quality slips or the price spirals out of line. If the consumer is indiscriminate, the producer is sorely tempted to by-pass the costly fine-tuning of his product.

The British, through their discriminating purchases, have been a major influence through several centuries in the development of a high standard of quality in the Bordeaux market. They had every reason to be annoyed by Americans who mindlessly jumped into the Bordeaux market recently, helping to force the price up beyond value-for-money and, in certain cases, the quality down.

There was a time when it was fashionable to sneer at California wine, without giving it so much as a fighting chance. By a curious irony, we are now becoming chauvinistic about California wine. If this attitude is not checked, the result could be disastrous. The amount of exceptionally fine wine being made in California today is small by comparison with European fine wines. Although we are fortunate in having plenty of good, sound beverage wine, truly exceptional in its class and price range, the production of premium wine has been understandably slow to meet demand. If the American consumer ignores the many exceptional values in imported premium wine, and forces up the price of California wines beyond reasonable value-for-money, he is simply letting himself become vulnerable to price-gouging producers, merchants and speculators. The market for California wine will become badly distorted (in many respects it is already). There will be short terms gains in profits, but in the long run, the consumer will become disenchanted with wine.

It has been proven beyond a doubt that wines of exceptional quality *can* be made in California. More and more consumers are at the point of proving to the producer that they have developed the sensitivity to recognize special quality and are willing to pay a reasonably higher price for higher quality.

Wine of special quality simply cannot be mass produced. The smaller, privately owned wineries which are staffed by the new generation of winemakers are as likely to make exceptional wine as the larger wineries with a great deal of financial backing and a battery of sophisticated equipment. One of the major and necessary ingredients in a fine wine is patient, attentive—even loving—care of the wines as they are developing. This is something which neither money nor expensive equipment can provide.

The California wine industry is going through a traumatic phase of its growth at the moment. As production is going from short supply to surplus, the market for California wine is undergoing a major change from a seller's to a buyer's market. Producer, distributor and merchant need to re-think their entire attitude toward marketing California wine. Admittedly, the problems are very complex. Distribution, through channels other than the wine merchant, has been very sloppy. Are the liquor distributors concerned that if wine *really* becomes popular, it will eat into their more profitable liquor market? Only Gallo, which distributes its own wines, seems to be doing a planned, aggressive job.

On the other hand, because of the abundance of grapes, the winemaker is more in a position to demand better quality grapes and thus make better quality wines. The consumer is also in a position to demand and get wines of exceptional quality and value. Provided the consumer uses great care and discrimination in his choices and leaves mediocre, over priced wines to die on the shelves; we can be reasonably assured that California will finally come to realize its potential as one of the great wine producing areas of the world.

Reflections on Wine Tasting

Two

Touring in the south of France for the first time several years ago, I was struck by a simple revelation—"This countryside looks like it stepped out of a Cézanne landscape!" I had been looking at Cézanne's great paintings of the Midi countryside as masterpieces of technique—extraordinary lighting, a fascinating play of perspective, line and brush strokes of muted, dusty greens and terra cotta orange. I realized then that they were also a remarkably complete expression of the actual natural landscape. Cézanne achieved it by a near mystic assimilation of his artistic vision and the landscape of the Midi.

Fine wine is no less the result of a total understanding and utilization of the possibilities of the natural environment in which the grape is produced, as well as a complete mastery of winemaking technique. The total complex of environmental factors (soil components, water supply, drainage, slope, heat, sunlight, rain and the general idiosyncrasies of weather) will find its way into the finished wine, shaping its identity. The winemaker has to have an intimate understanding of these factors and utilize them to the fullest advantage in order to produce the best wine possible. And yet, the winemaker does considerably more than guide the complex of natural processes through to some inevitable conclusion. He makes artistic decisions which affect the style and character of the wine. By managing the fermentation in one way or another he develops a particular style of wine. By following one option, the wine might be lighter, more quickly maturing; by following another, the wine will be more deeply flavored, and longer lasting. By his choice or avoidance of any of several optional cellar treatments, by blending various wines, by his choice of cooperage, by the attention and care he gives to the young wine as it develops, he breeds character into the wine, reflecting his personal taste.

Of course, we who enjoy his products are not out in the vineyards or down in his cellars, constantly looking over the winemaker's shoulder. The only evidence we have is the actual taste of the wine. In order to understand the ways in which the natural environment puts its stamp on the wine, and the ways in which the winemaker has crafted his wine, we must become reflective wine tasters. We have to take stock of the way that *we* perceive and enjoy his products and the qualities he has bred into them.

This chapter contains some basic reflections on the art of tasting and enjoying wine. My objective here is to develop a few guidelines by which one can direct one's perception toward quality factors in wine. These reflections will be carried into the following chapter in which I discuss the perception of qualities in wine which result from the effects of environment and the ways in which the grapes are grown. And in chapter four, I will discuss those quality factors which derive from the technique of winemaking.

Both amateur and connoisseur alike have a total impression of a wine and an immediate enjoyment or dislike. The difference is that for the amateur, it remains just that, a general impression of a beverage. For the connoisseur, it is a complex of quality factors which have been given balance and appeal by the art of the winemaker.

Most of us are enthusiastic amateurs who enjoy wine and have some notion of the wide range of differences between different wines. We are seeking a viable framework to give our wine drinking experience some kind of organization. We want to know what to look for in a fine wine.

Most of us recognize that some sort of analysis of our wine experience is necessary and inevitable. Almost any person who enjoys good table wine is aware that there are three "stages" in tasting and enjoying wine: visual examination of color and clarity, smelling the aroma and bouquet of the wine, and, finally, the actual tasting of the wine on the palate. These are the three "first principles" of tasting and enjoying wine, recognized almost universally by experienced wine drinkers. It is a major step in the right direction to have analyzed one's sensations of wine at least to that extent and to have made it a habit to take conscious notice of the three when one tastes or drinks wine. Beyond that point, it is not easy to find universal agreement among writers and connoisseurs when they further analyze sensory experiences of wine. Unfortunately, the language of sensory analysis which the amateur finds in literature on wine tasting seems at first like so much nonsense and verbage which he has great difficulty connecting with personal wine experience. The willing amateur is lost in a jungle of words.

This may be true, but the amateur should understand that wine is a complex subject matter which *demands* a special vocabulary. Ordinary wines do not inspire much comment, but there is always a great deal to say about very fine wine. Wine language fixes quality factors in one's mind so that they can be analyzed, described and discussed intelligently. One can share one's impressions of a wine with others. A wine drinker is not at the mercy of his or her purely subjective, hedonistic assessments. Being conversant in the language of wine, a person can *buy* wine more intelligently, simply because he can articulate his preferences and tastes to a knowledgeable merchant. There is also a great advantage in being able to understand skilled professionals such as Harry Waugh, Michael Broadbent, Karl Petrowsky and Robert Finigan who are experts in the art of using wine language meaningfully and succinctly.

There are two important and highly influential books which have been written on wine tasting: *Modern Sensory Methods of Evaluating Wine* by Professors M. A. Amerine, E. B. Roessler, and F. Filipello, and Michael Broadbent's *Wine Tasting*. Both of these books were written by professional wine people who are not primarily concerned with the problems of the aspiring amateur. Their point of view is conditioned by tasting objectives which are perhaps not of immediate interest to the ultimate consumer and enjoyer of the wine. The Amerine-Roessler-Filipello work, for example, is directed more toward winemakers, wine chemists and judges at state fairs. The point of view of Michael Broadbent is conditioned by his responsibility to make prognostications on the future of young wine and for buying and selling wine on a commercial scale. The amateur is not in the least interested in Michael Broadbent's views on how to make sales presentations of wines.

Modern Sensory Methods of Evaluating Wine was written at a time (1959) when California commercial wineries had a very lazy attitude toward sensory examination and analysis of their own wines. The objective of the book was to structure the attitude toward sensory analysis at the wineries when there was very little to begin with. It had a profoundly positive effect at the time and is still a very useful book. I doubt, however, that the authors intended it to be the ultimate word for the consumer on wine tasting and the aesthetic assessment of wine. Professor Amerine's superb essay, *Flavor as a Value*[1], would seem to indicate that.

Modern Sensory Methods of Evaluating Wine defines and analyzes several important quality factors in wine and then outlines a complex scheme for judging wine at state fairs. The judging scheme assigns a specific number of points for each of several quality factors and various points against the wines for various blemishes or flaws. It had the limited objective of encouraging technical proficiency at commercial wineries. It also served as an important tool for the wine chemist to use in assessing the basic soundness of a wine and the presence or absence of any obvious disorders. From the *consumer's* point of view, the judging scheme is so mathematical and rigid and the viewpoint so external, that one is reminded of the way in which cattle are judged at state fairs and the way that dogs and cats are judged at pet shows.

Unfortunately, *Modern Sensory Methods of Evaluating Wine* has become the gospel on the subject at the University of California. Other writers have taken this "judging" scheme over without giving it any kind of critical

---

[1] The essay appears in *Food and Civilization*, by S. M. Farber, N. L. Wilson, and R. H. L. Wilson; published by Charles C. Thomas, Springfield, Illinois (1966).

scrutiny. They have made the assumption that the best way for the amateur to learn about wine is to learn to "score" wines in the same manner that a state fair judge scores wines. For those amateurs who wish to taste wine as practice for becoming state fair judges, I can heartily recommend this method![1]

Aesthetic evaluation and enjoyment of wine has nothing whatsoever to do with assigning numbers to quality factors. "Value" in wine or art in general does not mean *numerical* value. Aesthetic perception is not a summation of the parts, but an active integration of the parts. One does not assess a painting by assigning so many points for composition, so many for use of color, so much for interpretation of subject matter, so many points for dexterity of brush-stroke, etc.[2] Granted, one recognizes these various aspects and looks at them systematically but it is the way that they are *interrelated* that creates the excitement and enjoyment of fine painting. The work should make a balanced, integrated statement. The same is true of wine.

By what right does anyone "legislate" either the actual number of quality factors which a person might discern in wine or their value in relation to one another? Any attempt to do so denies the fundamental freedom and heterogeneity of matters of taste. Any person who allows his taste to be molded in such a rigid manner is simply giving up that fundamental freedom and creating major blind spots in his perception of fine wine. One might well ask whether or not this "score card" method is an attempt to mold public taste so that it will accept and be completely content with commercial grade wine.

---

[1] The official score card breaks down as follows: appearance (2 points); color (2 points); aroma and bouquet (4 points); acescence, i.e. lack of vinegariness (2 points); total acid (2 points); sugar (1 point); body (1 point); flavor (2 points); astringency (2 points); general quality (2 points).

[2] How could a person "judge" the works of Frank Stella or Barnett Newman by using such

Michael Broadbent's *Wine Tasting* is perhaps the most useful book on the subject. It contains an extensive list of wine tasting terms with clear and concise working definitions along with a discussion of the most important quality factors. But the amateur needs considerably more than a good set of definitions. An amateur can sit tasting a wine for hours and might never be able, on his own, to analyze such things as acidity, earthiness, alcoholic "body", breeding or the lack of it, flavors derived from oak, etc.

Professor Amerine suggests that one should look for a mentor to guide the development of one's palate. There is certainly some merit to this, but often there is simply no one with an experienced palate who can continually guide the amateur in his day to day tasting and enjoyment of wines. More often than not, it is a matter of the blind leading the blind. Furthermore, the development of one's taste in fine wine should be an independent, personal and creative endeavor.

There is one major difficulty in analyzing one's sensations of wine. The elements which can be distinguished in a sensory impression of a wine are not natural objects which can be isolated by a simple act of abstraction. Unlike natural objects, they cannot be identified by someone else pointing a finger at them. Quality factors in wine are like so many fish in the stream of immediate experience; they die very quickly once thay are out of water. They seem to elude the normal techniques of definition.

But an analysis of the sensory impression of a wine is not, on that account, hopelessly subjective either. Many of the basic elements in the *sensory* complex have their foundation in a *physio-chemical* complex of elements. These elements can be separated out by the chemical process of qualitative anlysis. Chemical analysis at least gives the assurance that there are some elements in the whole impression on which one can focus with some practice, that one is not pursuing a chimera. Chemical analysis tells us that there are so many basic elements in wine: water, alcohol (among which predominates ethanol, with lesser quantities of butanol, propanol, etc.), sugars (among which there are glucose, fructose, lactose, etc.), extract, acids (among which there are tartaric, malic, lactic, citric, etc.), esters, aldehydes, tannin, and other trace elements.

As one's skill and experience in wine tasting develops, it becomes increasingly helpful and interesting to check one's sensory evaluation against some of the basic results of the chemical analysis, if they are available (e.g., total acid, percentage of sugar, percentage of alcohol, extract content). But no amount of chemical analysis can help in an immediate way with one's sensory analysis. After all, if you think that you detect an aroma which reminds you of roses or crushed raspberries, you can hardly run out to the corner chemist to have him analyze the wine and verify your impressions. The impression can be quite real, particularly if the aroma is distinct and persistent enough and if other people can recognize it. An astute wine chemist might even be able to isolate the chemical trace element which gave rise to the sensory element. But if the trace element cannot be found, this does not necessarily make your impression any less real.

Wine is not merely the sum of chemical elements. Wine is called a "living thing", which is to say that its elements are organically interrelated. Wine is an extension of natural processes, guided and controlled by human art. The *aesthetic* perception and analysis of wine is one thing; the *chemical* analysis of wine is quite another.

We need a more pragmatic approach to the sensory analysis of wine and the use we make of wine language. The great spokesman for American common sense, William James, taught that if the word you are using has any meaning, do not assume that its correct definition in terms of other words is necessarily going to tell *me* what you are talking about. Rather, if your word means something, show me how I can get in or around or up to whatever it is referring to so that I, too, can have an experience of it. Most wine writers fail to emphasize the most fundamental technique of sensory analysis of wines, the one which follows James' advice and is easily accessible to the amateur. *If one wishes to focus on an element in the sensory complex of a wine, one should compare a wine which has a significant level of that particular element with another wine which has only low levels of that element but is similar in other respects.* Not only will the positive *presence* of the element appear in bold relief, but one can see what sensory difference its *not* being there makes. It is not so much a matter of *analysis* as it is a matter of *perception*; and effective perception needs the right point of perspective which side by side comparison provides.

For example, if one is vague about the meaning of "acidity" in wine, one could compare, say, a lower acid California Sauvignon Blanc or Grenache Rosé from the San Joaquin Valley with a higher acid wine of the same variety from Napa or Sonoma. In order to get a better idea of what experienced wine tasters mean by "body", one could compare two Chardonnays from California's Napa Valley, one with high alcohol and the other with normal or low alcohol. Drinking two different vintages of the same wine simultaneously is always very interesting and instructive. This not only gives one perspective on the effects which different weather patterns have on the same wines of different vintage, it also gives one perspective on the differences which age makes on similar wines.

The professional taster has an extensive wine-memory from which he can make comparisons. The amateur does not have this extensive memory backlog. He needs the perspective which side by side comparisons provide. The consumer does not have to wait for a mentor, a wine appreciation class or a wine tasting session to learn about wine. Learning, enjoyment, quality comparison for personal preference, all can proceed side by side.

The mechanics of this system are not as difficult and impractical as they may seem. Instead of ordering or serving a single fifth of wine, order or serve a pair of contrasting half-bottles. If half-bottles of some wines are not available for home consumption, decant half of the full bottle into an empty half-bottle, which can then be recorked and stored in the refrigerator where it will keep reasonably well for several weeks. If it is done carefully enough so that very little air is left between the wine and the cork, refrigeration is not necessary. Better yet, have enough people on hand for dinner so that two or three contrasting wines can be served simultaneously. The possibilities are endless and fascinating. But the main point to the system is that it puts the amateur on his way to understanding quality in wine. I have serious doubts whether quality has anything to do with ranking on an abstract, numerical scale. It is certain, however, that the constant comparison of wines develops one's perception of those qualities which an expert winemaker painstakingly breeds into his wines.

The situation in California is particularly advantageous for comparison tastings which throw quality factors into focus. Most California winemakers are open minded and experimental. Often a winemaker will have difficulty choosing between two options in making the same wine so he will create two lots of the same wine, one which followed the first option (e.g., filtering or fining or aging in *French* oak) and one which followed the second option (no filtering, no fining, or aging in *American* oak). Comparing these two wines side by side can be tremendously instructive and can help one immeasurably in building up concepts of quality factors. In California, we have had examples of two different winemakers making wine from grapes grown in the same vineyard, sometimes in the same vintage year. Tasting such wines together can give one an excellent idea of the effect which different styles of winemaking have on wine. Of course, if you have a rapport with an intelligent and informed wine merchant, he can help you set up interesting comparisons.

For centuries, Frenchmen have been enjoying a white wine made from Chardonnay grapes fermented in oak and aged in oak. In California, we not only have Chardonnay which is made in this manner, but also Chardonnay which is fermented in stainless steel, with all further processing done without contact with wood. The Frenchman has virtually no perspective from which his palate can focus on either the Chardonnay character or the oak character of the wine. As the Californian tastes his two Chardonnays against each other, the fruit character of his oakless Chardonnay will come through clear, unencumbered and assertive, against the complexity of the Chardonnay with oak. Reversing the point of view, the oak character of the latter will stand out in bold relief against the varietal purity of the former. The Californian is in a position to understand how the winemaker has balanced the Chardonnay character against the oak character and to enjoy the interplay of the two characters on the palate. His next *French* Chardonnay might be quite a revelation!

Instead of setting out a list of wine tasting terms and definitions, it is my intention throughout the next two chapters, to explain various quality factors in wine by associating them with the conditions under which they are developed and by suggesting various side by side tasting comparisons which will give the perspective necessary to perceive them.

From this point of side by side comparison one can go on to build what Michael Broadbent calls a "vinous memory". As he also recommends, some sort of *"aide memoire"* is essential—a tasting notebook, cellar book, or card system. This is one further means of extending the technique of comparison tasting to tastings which are widely separated in time. The discipline of writing down one's impressions will repress the tendency toward the more subjective flights of fancy which fine wine is apt to inspire. Keeping a cellar book is no mere pedantic exercise but a tremendous help in developing one's palate. By reading through one's notes occasionally, it is fascinating to watch how the palate develops and becomes more perceptive. The palate is not a passive, rigidly unchanging sensory organ. The art lover develops his eye for paintings and the music lover develops his ear for music; so too, one develops one's palate for wine tasting. The more diverse one's reflective wine tasting experience becomes, the more individual and complex will become each new wine tasting as it is set off against the developing background of past wine tasting experience.

Maintaining a cellar book will also help in developing an understanding of how wine has a life and develops in the bottle. By tasting a bottle of the same wine once every year or so, making notes at each tasting, valuable understanding of how wine improves, reaches a peak and declines can be gained. From just such experiences one can build up an ability to make prognostications on the future of young wine. The ability to make such judgments should not be the exclusive province of professional tasters.

The world of wine is so exciting, so fecund with possibility, with so much fine wine turning up in the most unsuspected places, one should not be disconcerted by the preoccupation which some people have with deductive wine games, as though it were the pinnacle of wine culture to be able to deduce the identity of a wine in a blind tasting. More often than not, this is symptomatic of a palate which is experienced to the point of being jaded. Deduction goes on in a hypothetically closed, discrete universe where all tastes are known previously and related *inter se*. Nothing really new is learned by playing deductive games, but deduction does serve the very legitimate purpose of sharpening one's existing stock of knowledge. Nevertheless, in the very open world of California wines, in which we are just beginning to realize so many possibilities, with so many fine new vineyards just coming into production, such deductive game-playing should not be accorded a very high priority.

Michael Broadbent (in *Wine Tasting*) makes the interesting assertion that from the sight and smell of a wine alone one can extrapolate to its taste. There seems to be some controversy over the point. Professor Amerine, for example, disagrees. There is no question that one can draw a great many conclusions about how a wine will taste, simply by examining color and bouquet. Here one must understand the conditions of professional wine tasting. Often faced with the responsibility of evaluating an extensive range of absolutely first-rate French or German wines (often as many as fifty at a time!) in such a context, it is inevitable that sight and smell should become most important. The professional taster *has* to develop an ability to make accurate deductions. But in the experience of the average wine lover, bouquet is so much an invitation to taste the wine; the rhythm of eye, to nose, to palate is so much an integral part of the aesthethic enjoyment of wine, that to interpose an elaborate deduction between nose and taste seems to me to be a rather pedantic exercise. Of what possible use could such a scheme be to the non-professional lover of fine wine?

As far as the consumer/wine lover is concerned, there are several basic functions of wine tasting: first, to understand and appreciate how wine is a reflection of the land, the climate, the overall weather of the vintage year, and the type of grape; second, to participate in the winemaker's art; third, to appreciate whatever there is of quality in the wine, aside from personal preferences; fourth, to assess the overall quality and appeal of the wine, its aging potential, and value for money; and fifth, to make some estimation as to the use of the wine at one's dinner, luncheon or cocktail table.

All too often, tasters are overly preoccupied with the question of *ranking* wines, trying to force wines into some "objective" hierarchy, based on an "ideal" of what a wine-type should be. To have a fixed ideal of what a wine-type should be like and "judge" wines according to the way they approach that ideal, is surely one of the most naive ways to approach fine wine. The world of wine is simply too rich and fecund for such a narrow approach. Of course, for those who prefer *ideal* wines, I can only say *"Chacun son goût"*—every man to his taste! I myself prefer wines that I can drink.

The preoccupation with "scoring" wines has led to an attitude which treats wine tastings as though they were akin to competitive games of sport. Often, a wine placed down on the list because of some minor flaw would be an absolutely first-rate match for some particular entree; or perhaps it is a very distinctive, individual wine which merits special attention in spite of its flaws. Perhaps the wine is so tannic and "dusty" that it is virtually untastable—but take a look at the wine in five years and it might turn out to be your favorite Cabernet Sauvignon! Perhaps a wine has an exceptional flavor and superb sugar/acid balance—"Woops, sorry! We only allow two points for flavor and, let me see, sugar/acid balance doesn't seem to be on the list, sorry!"—or perhaps the wine is going through an awkward phase or perhaps the luck of the draw produced a poor bottle. One will occasionally run across tasting notes which are so completely contrary to personal experience that either of the latter two must have been the case.

Blind tasting can be tremendously instructive and enjoyable and an excellent opportunity to assess the rarer or more costly wines which are not generally available at tasting rooms. A blind tasting should ideally consist of several wines of similar type. "Blind", of course, means that the bottles are covered or the wines are decanted so that their identity is hidden—not so much for the guessing game purposes as to dispel any preconceived notions which would prevent impartial assessment of the wine. One should not feel constrained to exchange social pleasantries, but should concentrate on assessing the wines at hand.

Rather than discussing the wines immediately, the procedure in California, at least, is to have each taster make his own notes on each wine. Here it is useful to assess the appearance of all the wines, followed by assessments and notes on their bouquet, followed by successive tasting of the wines. A spitoon should be provided and used, so that the characteristics of each wine will be kept distinct. I find it useful to check one's notes by re-examining each individual wine according to appearance, bouquet and taste. Here it is important to assess the interplay of all the quality factors and to *integrate* (not add) all the qualities of the wine. One should take an educated guess at the identity of the wine (particularly if it is a significant wine of special quality) and make a note of it.

Ranking the wines is interesting because it enables one to compare some of the criteria and value systems other wine tasters use to evaluate the wines. A simple scale of 20 seems to be the most comfortable, with exceptionally fine wine scoring 17–20; basically sound wines with no major defects, 13–16; and poor to ordinary wines, 0–12.

Following the tasting, a comparison of notes can be very enlightening and cause for lively discussion. One taster will often have an unusual point of view, picking out qualities which others overlooked. Following the tasting of the wines, it is interesting to drink the remainder of the wines with appropriate foods. Often a wine which was not so attractive in the tasting will show very well against a particular food. The final criterion, after all, is whether the wine is enjoyable in its proper context—as an integral part of the art of the table.

Viticulture and the Quality of Wine

Three

There is an interesting piece of folk wisdom about wine which many writers seize upon and blow up into an explanation of the relation between environment and the quality of wine. It is what I call the "myth of the struggling vine", curiously akin to the equally nonsensical "myth of the struggling artist". The myth states that only abject deprivation will generate quality in the end product of the vine, that the vine must "struggle" to achieve greatness. Some writers carry the myth further, saying that because the vine undergoes frequent battering from the unstable weather conditions in European vineyards, only to come around to producing great wines when the conditions are perfect, the bad year is a necessary condition for the good year, that the bad year gives the vines a chance to "rest" (poor things!) and prepare for the task of producing great grapes the following year. There is certainly a kernel of truth in this folk wisdom, but the myth is a classic example of anthropomorphic thinking. If the vines have to "struggle" unsuccessfully against a devastating September rain storm, they do not set their "minds" to doing a better job the following year. Such an occurrence is indeed a tragedy for the grower, the winemaker and the wine lover; but the vines do not undergo a catharsis as a result of the tragedy.

What is even more disconcerting is that some writers draw a "conclusion" from the myth, arguing that because of the relatively stable weather conditions in California, one must expect a ho-hum succession of good enough vintages, but never any peaks and valleys, never any heights. Reasonable and open minded people know that experience has proven otherwise.

The word "struggle" puts the whole question in the wrong light. There are perhaps no more healthy vines than those grown on difficult terrain. Unhealthy, "struggling" vines and plant organisms of *any* kind, by the most uncompromising rule of nature, are particularly subject to plant disease and attack by plants pests (a kind of rude law of survival) and will eventually die.

On the other hand, vines which produce quality wines generally undergo certain beneficial forms of *stress*: reasonably severe pruning, lack of fertilizer, restricted water supply, lack of richly fertile soil, etc. Other forms of stress—gusty spring winds which damage the canes, excessive heat especially during the ripening period, heavy rains during the harvest—are unfortunate occurrences which have no beneficial effects whatsoever.

It is important to distinguish the various forms of stress, both beneficial and harmful, and understand the effect which each of these has on the quality of the wines.

There is simply no getting around the complexity of the relationship between the culture of the vine and the ultimate quality of the wine.

There are two sides to the environment of the grape vine, namely, the *soil* (which involves the actual mineral-organic makeup of the soil, moisture and such soil characteristics as heat retention, porosity, drainage, slope) and *climate* (sunshine, rain, wind, and the heat of the air which surrounds the vines). Through the medium of the *soil*, the roots of the vine absorb water, minerals and other nutriments and trace elements necessary for the proper development of the trunk, branches, foliage and the grape. Within the soil structure itself, moisture, heat and oxygen are needed to break down soil minerals into nutriments which can be absorbed by the root structure. *Climatic* conditions furnish the foliage of the vine with the basic energy forms of heat and sunlight which are converted into sugar in the process known as photosynthesis. During the ripening period, this sugar, in solution, is translocated from the leaves through the vine to the fruit. The object of viticulture is to produce fruit which has a correct balance of water, sugar, acid (of which more later) and fruit extract.

Water serves in two capacities: first, it is a necessary element in the development of vine and foliage (both as a carrier of nutriments in solution and as a constituent) and second, it is an element in the development of the berry (both as a constituent of the berry and as a carrier of sugars, nutriments and trace elements necessary for berry structure and extract). The *amount* of water supply has one very important effect on the quality of the finished wine. An over-abundant water supply will increase the water and the sugar content of the berry at the expense of fruit extract. Given sufficient sunlight and heat, enough sugar can be produced to match the water content of the berries, even in vines which are heavily laden with fruit. Production per acre will be high. However, the amount of fruit extract which the vines can produce from elements in the soil is considerably more constant. The ratio of extract to water and sugar will be low and the wine made from the grapes will tend to be low in flavor intensity.

In Europe, when there are two or three *highly productive* years in a row, the quality in the second and third years seems to receed. This is not because the vines lack "rest", but because production is outstripping the ability of the vines to produce concentrated extract.

Extract is a fundamental quality factor in grapes and in wines. Chemically, wine extract is defined as the total soluble solids which remain after water, alcohol and sugars are taken from the wine. This can be measured as a percentage of total volume. In sensory analysis, this translates into fullness and complexity of flavor and has its foundation in the amount and complexity of extract, although not *all* extract is a basis for flavor.

Flavor is the most important element in the complex experience we have of food and wine. It involves both the sense of taste and the sense of smell, being a complex, overall sensation which arises from our perception and integration of tastes and smells. Flavor is an aesthetic matter; the awareness and realization of flavor is learned through experience. An exceptionally fine, well flavored wine is lost on a very inexperienced palate.

Wines which are more deeply and intensely flavored contain greater extract and are generally more costly to make. It is important to understand the basis of flavor in wine so that one can assess value-for-money in wine.

Vines which produce grapes for highly flavored, fine quality wines need a soil complex which will supply the proper amount of water, nutrition and extract building elements for the fruit. This is possible in any of hundreds of different soil/terrain combinations. Hillside plantings have definite advantages; viz., the very slope of the hill assures good drainage and prevents the water supply from becoming excessive and thus lowering extract. Good drainage, however, can occur in relatively flat vineyards where the soil is porous. The soil in the Napa Valley (California) floor is based on very porous, pulverized volcanic debris. Soils in the Medoc (Bordeaux) are made up, generally, of various mixtures of sand and gravel with elements of clay and loam also present in varying degrees. Soil in the Livermore Valley of California and the Graves district of Bordeaux is extremely gravelly.

Grape vines make very definite demands with regard to the way they receive their water supply. Ideally, a vineyard should receive most of its water supply during the winter when the vines are dormant. (The vines make significant growth only when the average daytime and nightime temperature is above 50°.) Ideally, the growing season should be virtually free of rain. Summer rains encourage molds to form on the fruit. Most such molds will simply rot and destroy the grapes. Non-irrigated vineyards need at least two feet of rain per year in order to be commercially feasible. But production can be greatly increased by irrigation. In fact, irrigation can increase yield per acre by as much as two or three times, though the wines will definitely suffer in terms of flavor intensity. On the other hand, wines from irrigated vineyards can be quite sound and palatable as a beverage, and the price will be proportionately lower (i.e., by one half to two-thirds lower). Obviously, there is plenty of room for both elegant costly premium wines and for ordinary inexpensive beverage wines. Few of us have either the budget or the inclination to maintain a strict diet of elaborately prepared foods accompanied by appropriately elegant wines.

Irrigation is not *necessarily* detrimental to flavor intensity and quality. In vineyards where the annual rainfall is far below normal, irrigation which compensates for the lack of rain will not have an adverse effect on quality. In fact, a producer of some of the finest California white wine, Chalone Vineyards (Monterey County), uses a system of drip irrigation. In normal irrigation, the topsoil is flooded along furrows which run between the rows of vines. In drip irrigation, water enters the soil at a single point near the base of each vine, in a slow, unrelenting drop-by-drop manner. The water supply gets through to the subsoil without absorbing the more organic elements in the topsoil. Drip irrigation is often referred to as "ideal average rainfall". In the case of Chalone, it merely compensates for an abnormally low annual rainfall.

It is important to recognize quality differences which derive from productivity of vines. Less experienced wine drinkers should make careful comparisons between, for example, less expensive, but sound, bulk wines from the highly productive San Joaquin Valley with wines from producers who have a reputation for intensely flavored wines; e.g., Mayacamas, Sterling or Freemark Abbey (all Napa). One can taste *into* these latter; there is intensity and nuance. The San Joaquin Valley wine will be sound, perhaps even as drinkable, but it is monochromatic, unexciting when one scrutinizes it carefully. The Napa wines might be made from vines which produced two to four tons to the acre while the San Joaquin Valley wines are made from vines which produce nine to twelve tons per acre. Naturally, the former will be more expensive.

Thanks to a remarkable wine technology, California produces an abundance of good, wholesome, inexpensive beverage wine made from grapes grown in highly productive vineyards. Many of these wines are a pleasure to drink as an accompaniment to basic, everyday American foods: hamburger sandwiches, fried chicken, grilled chops, etc. These beverage wines can be quite satisfying and provide everything one would want from a wine in the context. Learning to enjoy these simple wines provides a good foundation and perspective from which to develop a keener appreciation of the more costly premium wines.

In assesing wines, consumers should avoid using a single rigid scale of values and the habit of ranking wines on an absolute scale. The wine drinker should adjust his wine values and expectations according to the intention of the winemaker, the use he plans to make of the wine and the price he is willing to pay.

The *age* of the vines is very important. As the vines mature through several decades, they develop deep and massive root structures. This makes available ample supplies of those elements which are necessary for the development of full, complex extract in wine. Young vines feed on a shallower stratum of soil and produce both less extract and less complexity of extract. Older vines seem to produce wines of greater complexity of flavor. This is one of the reasons why European wines are often more complex than California wines. Older vines do not *necessarily* produce wines of greater complexity, however. There are other quality factors involved.

In California, it is difficult to track down wines which are made from older vines because there is a considerable amount of blending of wines from newer and older vines (understandably!). Two of the finest Petite Sirahs made in California (Ridge York Creek 1971 and Freemark Abbey 1969) came from Fritz Maytag's ninety year old vines on Spring Mountain (Napa). Both wines are extraordinarily rich and complex. Zinfandels with the appellation "Deaver Ranch, Amador" (Harbor Winery, Sutter Home Winery, Corti Brothers or Gemello's) are made from very old vines and might be used for comparison.

Another major factor in the development of extract in wine is the degree of sweetness of the grapes when they are picked. We will consider this further along in our discussion.

Good drainage is one very definite check on the productivity of the vine. But different *grape varieties* are also structured to be more or less productive. As a general rule, the varieties which are naturally less prolific will produce a wine of higher quality. Grape varieties such as French Colombard or Carignane will produce anywhere from seven to twelve tons of grapes per acre while the vines of the varieties Chardonnay and Cabernet Sauvignon may produce from one to four tons per acre.[1]

Many Californians are regular tasters at various wineries so that they have an idea of varietal differences. An interesting comparison might be made by comparing varietal wines of Paul Masson or Almaden with a comparable range from Sebastiani (Sonoma). The former tend to be highly blended so that differences are not very distinct. The latter have honest and richly varied varietal characteristics (and, incidentally, are more attractively priced).

Pruning is another means of controlling the productivity of the vine. This is certainly one of the areas where the human artistic factor can affect quality. Experience has shown how mid-winter cutting back of the dormant vines can regulate the number of grape clusters which a vine will produce. Highly concentrated wines are made from vines which are pruned back so far that they produce less than a few bottles of wine per vine. What is lost in quantity is gained in the intensity of flavor and varietal character.

---

[1] There has been a great deal of "clonal selection" in California—selecting and propagating strains of Chardonnay, Cabernet and Pinot Noir which are highly productive. The consumer has to rely on the sensitivity of his palate and on careful comparisons. He should not object too strongly, so long as higher productivity is reflected in a considerably lower price.

Such careful pruning will especially benefit the premium grape varietals; heavy pruning of a common variety such as Carignane would only result in a highly concentrated ordinary wine.

The vintage year 1961 in Bordeaux and the year 1970 in California were peculiar cases in which early frosts acted as "natural pruning agents". The frosts destroyed a good many early buds, leaving only a few clusters per vine to mature. The 1961 Bordeaux Reds have an extraordinary intensity and complexity of flavor, but not at the expense of balance and elegance. Some of the 1970 Cabernets in California seem to be headed in the general direction of great intensity. Of course, intensity of flavor does not necessarily guarantee the ultimate quality of the wine. In the final analysis the wines must be balanced.

Pruning can also work in the opposite direction. By leaving a considerable number of buds on the dormant vines, a heavy growth of vine will result, producing an over-abundance of berry clusters. This practice is called "over-cropping" and is perhaps the worst enemy of quality in wine.

French wines with the designation *"appelation contrôlée* come from vineyards in which production is kept below certain legal limits through careful pruning. In California one has to rely on the reputation of the winery and the sensitivity of one's palate. Less scrupulous wine producers in California are understandably very aggressive in their opposition to any *"appellation contrôlée"* laws which might limit productivity. Perhaps it is time for American consumers to speak out in favor of *"appellation contrôlée"* laws for American premium wines.

Although most flavor in wine is derived from fruit extract, there are other flavor characteristics which derive from the soil and differ from each other according to differences in the makeup of the soil. This is called "earthiness" or *"goût de terroir"*, a French wine term which, roughly translated, means "a tang or flavor of the soil". Where these flavor characteristics are particularly strong, I prefer to use the term "earthy"; where the flavors are more subtle and kept in balance with fruit, I prefer to use to term *"goût de terroir"*, although in common wine parlance they are the same term.

Earthiness is not a particularly elusive, esoteric characteristic in wine, requiring some arcane sixth sense to recognize it. Rich, moist topsoil has a very distinct aroma. Anyone can verify this by simply scooping up a handful of moist topsoil and smelling it. Fine French Red Burgundy will sometimes have a distinct aroma of humus. Heavier aromas of this sort often find their way into bulk wines which come from the irrigated vineyards on the valley floors. Compare, for example, an earthy Zinfandel from Italian Swiss Colony or Gallo with a very fruity Zinfandel from Louis Martini to get some idea of earthiness. In the case of bulk wines from irrigated vineyards, the irrigation encourages the roots to feed on the higher stratum of soil with the consequent proliferation of strong earth flavors, and at the same time increases the water-to-extract ratio in the grapes with the consequent loss of fruit extract, which would counterbalance the earthiness. In vineyards where fertilizer has been used in more than the most judicious quantities, the aroma and taste of fertilizer will often come through in the wine.

Vineyards which are planted on hillsides or on flat terrain which has good drainage are less liable to produce very earthy wines. Hillside terrain avoids large deposits of rich topsoil, while well drained bottom land sends the roots deep and away from topsoil. In premium quality wine, flavors which can be assigned to the effect of soil makeup are generally and intentionally very subtle. Only a great deal of comparative tasting will enable one to properly isolate and identify these flavors.

The gravelly soil of the Livermore Valley in California and the Graves district of Bordeaux imparts a very subtle but distinct *goût de terrior* which one can only describe as gravelly. Volcanic soil imparts a very distinct *goût de terroir*. Without the aid of comparison tasting, it is very difficult to focus on these characteristics. A very interesting comparison tasting might consist of several white wines made from Sauvignon Blanc grapes: Wente Brothers Sauvignon Blanc from the gravelly soils of the Livermore Valley, Spring Mountain or Oakville Sauvignon Blanc from the volcanic soil of the Napa Valley, the Sauvignon Blanc of Gallo, made predominately from grapes which are grown in the sandy soil of the San Joaquin Valley, and the white wine made at Margaux (Bordeaux) called "Pavillion Blanc", from soil which is a mixture of loam, clay and gravel.

Although fruit extract and trace elements derived from the soil are important factors which contribute to the flavor of wine, these elements must have a strong framework provided by alcohols, sugars and acids if the wine is to be successful.

These three factors (alcohol, sugar and acid) are dependent on the "other side" of the vine environment, namely, sunshine and the heat of the air which surrounds the vine.

Once the berry clusters have set in the spring and swelled to a certain point, they appear to remain in a state of suspended animation for several weeks. The berries are mouth-puckeringly acidic. Burgundians and others who live in viticultural areas often use the juice of unripened grapes (called "verjuice") as a substitute for vinegar. People who live in very hot climates have a habit of sucking the very tart, acidic juice from immature fruit as a means of assuaging thirst.

While the grape is in this relatively dormant state, the vines are transforming energy in the form of heat and solar radiation (sunlight) into another energy form: sugar. The sugar is stored in solution with the sap, which in turn is held in the trunk and the vines. As the mid-summer heat begins to dissipate the acid from the berries, they take on color and begin to swell. They develop a cellular structure which will absorb more and more of the sweetened sap of the vines.

There is an analogy to this stage in other fruits. At the beginning of the season for any fruit, some less scrupulous fruit growers, as soon as the fruit has the appearance of ripeness, will rush the premature fruit to market in order to gain a big price advantage. One is inevitably disappointed in buying this premature fruit. Although there is sufficient pigment to give the appearance of ripeness, the fruit is still tasteless and puckery with acid. Leaving it out in the sun to ripen does not improve matters. The acidity dissipates in the heat, but one is left with mealy, unappetizing flesh, with little of the sweet, succulent juice which one associates with tree ripened fruit. If the summer is cloudy and cool in the vineyards or there is danger of rains at harvest, some winemakers are forced to pick the grapes at this stage, but the resulting "green" wine will be disappointingly acidic and sharp and will never age into anything attractive.

Ideally, wine grapes should develop just enough sugar to produce a sufficient level of alcohol in the wine with just enough sugar left over to give the wine a bit of a smile. There is a type of alcohol which oenologists call "glycerol" which will give a dry wine a slightly sweet finish. Glycerol can be recognized by the "tears" which a wine will make as it slides down the side of a glass. Both the amount of alcohol and the amount of residual sugar will have a strong bearing on the style of the wine. The winemaker's decision of when to pick is absolutely crucial. The sugar content of the grapes at picking time is measured in terms of *degrees brix*. The degrees brix reading divided by two, will be roughly equal to the percentage of potential alcohol (+ residual sugar).

Acidity is an equally crucial quality factor in wine. With the residual sugar it provides a balancing framework for the basic flavor constituents of the wine. Acidity seems to provide a "backbone", or shall we say, structural soundness, to the wine. Rather like the squeeze of lemon that one adds to a piece of broiled fish—not so much for the lemon taste, as for the way it seems to throw the delicate flavor of the fish into relief. Low acid wines are flat and listless. They seem to die half-way across the palate. A wine with good acidity is refreshingly alive on the palate. The volatile (aroma/bouquet) aspects of the wine seem to be still intact by the time the wine reaches the back of the palate, near the "chimney" which leads to the olfactory sensors. One can locate this "chimney" by consciously producing the snoring noise; i.e., by inhaling through both the open mouth and the nose in such a way as to make a snoring noise. To increase the effect of the finish of a wine, one should exhale through the nose, *immediately* after swallowing the wine. A considerable amount of aromatic elements will be carried to the olfactory sensors and one will have a much better appreciation of the finish of the wine.

In general, a wine with good acidity will also have a good finish. Wine needs good acidity with respect to itself; *table* wine also needs good acidity with respect to the foods with which it is being served, in order that it help make *their* flavors alive on the palate and stimulate the flow of saliva and gastric juices so that one better digests the food. I will discuss this at greater length in the chapter on food and wine.

Oenologists recognize several kinds of acid which differ chemically (malic, tartaric, lactic, citric, acetic, etc.) but there is some dispute over whether there are significant sensory differences associated with all these different acids. The non-professional taster should not feel inadequate because he lacks the ability to distinguish the tastes of *all* acids which differ chemically. It seems that there *are* sensory differences and that a great deal of tasting experience will educate one to detect these differences. Malic acid, in a very young wine, is fairly easily recognized by the aroma and taste of raw cooking apples. Acetic acid (vinegar) has a distinct vinegar aroma—a trace of this is not necessarily unattractive in some wines; e.g., French Red Burgundy often has a trace of acetic acid.[1] Some California and Alsatian white wines which are beyond their prime will sometimes have an unat-

---

[1] Any trace of acetic acid is anathema to the mathematically oriented wine "judges" who abound in California. Score one point *for* jug burgundy and one point *against* a sublime old Chambertin!

tractive "grapefruit" taste which probably derives from citric acid. Generally, acidity is recognized by the "tartness" of the wine. It is a taste which plays a supporting role on the palate in the overall *flavor* of the wine.

Perhaps the best standard of comparison for acidity in wine is not California, but French and German wine. A good comparison tasting for acidity might be a California Johannisberg Riesling with a fine Moselle Riesling or perhaps a California Chardonnay with a French Chablis.

For the moment we want to understand what environmental conditions are conducive to good acidity. There has been a great deal of idle speculation and hypothesis in this area. Excessive sunlight is often named as the culprit responsible for reduced acidity in wines. This seemed not unreasonable since wines from very sunny locations seem generally less strong in acid than wines from the more cloudy northern European vineyards. Since California vineyards are blessed with sunshine days in almost uninterrupted succession, the inference was made that California would never produce wines of good acidity. They would always be somewhat flat by European standards. What had appeared as a blessing, was actually a strong liability.

In a masterpiece of viticultural research and experimentation, Professor Kliewer at the University of California at Davis subjected this hypothesis to a rigorous inquiry.[1] By an ingenious series of experiments he found that sunlight has little if anything to do with the dissipation of acidity from ripening wine grapes but that temperature is the controlling factor. The dissipation of acidity increases as temperature increases. This was not a total surprise to the oenologists at Davis, but rather a vindication of views they had held in the face of criticism.

This result underlines the importance of soil type as a heat retainer. In

---

[1] These experiments have been summarized by Dr. Kliewer in an ongoing series of articles for the *American Journal of Oenology and Viticulture*.

areas of the Côte d'Or, for example, where white wine grapes are grown in chalky soil, this soil type probably functions as an excellent heat retainer which helps to give the wine its attractive acidity. The slate soil of the Moselle and the rocky-pebbly soil of Châteauneuf-du-Pape seem to function in like manner. Any well drained soil (e.g., sandy, gravelly, volcanic, alluvial, etc.) has good heat retention capacity while soils rich in humus are highly moisture retentive, the moisture acting as a cooling influence, particularly at night. It seems that well-drained soils with good heat retention provided the vines with sufficient nightime heat to manufacture sugar, but not enough to effect significant dissipation of acidity.

Grape variety is another factor. Each grape variety seems to have its own appropriate range of heat regimen with respect to proper ripening and acidity retention. Even in hot environments, such varieties as Grenache, Grignolino, Zinfandel and French Colombard seem to retain a fair degree of acidity. The grape of French Red Burgundy (Pinot Noir), on the other hand, is exasperatingly temperamental about its heat regimen.

At the point of harvest, the winemaker has two primary concerns—the level of sugar in the grape (degrees brix) and the level of total acid (measured as a percentage per 100 cc.). The decision of when to pick is absolutely crucial to the art of winemaking. We will take up the consideration of that decision in the next chapter.

Winemaking and the Quality of

Wine

Four

I have compared the art of winemaking to the art of painting. Perhaps it also shares something of the art of water color. Like the water colorist, the winemaker has to work very quickly and be completely organized.

The actual winemaking process takes place in a relatively short time. Granted that the winemaker has quality grapes, the essential style of the wine is determined in the decision of when to pick, and in the crush and fermentation which follow immediately. He has not only to organize his equipment, but he must think through as much as possible the entire range of possibilities and his series of respones and adjustments to each set of possibilities. No fine, individual wine is made by following a rigid formula.

Winemaking is one of those things which looks so easy but is really a tremendously exacting art. There are literally hundreds of things which can be done or omitted inadvertantly which can mar the quality or show up as flaws in the end product.

Matters of a preventive nature are rather the specific business of the winemaker. The ability to discern flaws in the wine are neither the initial nor the primary concern of the amateur. It is far more important to understand exactly what the winemaker does in a positive way to effect quality and balance in the end product, how he develops a style of wine which is appropriate to the grapes with which he works. The ability to discern what a winemaker did with a wine develops as connoisseurship develops. God help the connoisseur who can only see what a winemaker did wrong with a wine!

The first and foremost decision the winemaker has to make is when to pick, for this decision will greatly affect the balance and character of the wine. It is not something which can be reduced to a formula. This is strictly an artistic decision—picking earlier might result in a lighter, more austere, perhaps elegant style; picking later might result in a softer, "fatter" style with richness of fruit. Of equal importance, the picking decision lays the foundation for the sugar/acid balance of the wine. Although there are ways in which it can be partially adjusted further down the line in the winemaking process, it is important that the foundations of a good sugar/acid balance be laid from the start.

In the autumn, as the sugar level rises and approaches the level of ripeness which the winemaker prefers, the acidity respires from the grape at a rate which is directly related to the heat. The winemaker has to watch *very* carefully, testing at least once a week. The ideal for most winemaking would be, say, a sugar reading between 22 and 26 degrees brix and a relatively high acid, say, .75 to 1.1. This is possible when there is a delicate balance of weather conditions during the ripening period; i.e., warm enough to develop sugar, but not so warm as to dissipate acid very rapidly. Vineyards planted on hillsides are perhaps most desirable for this purpose. The excellent air circulation through hillside vineyards helps to protect the fruit from excessively high temperatures which would dissipate acidity.

Assuming that acidity is maintained at reasonable levels, there are significant sensory differences in wines made from grapes picked at different degrees of sugar. High sugar produces high alcohol in wine. The *sensory* effect of alcohol in wine is called the *body* of the wine. There seems to be some disagreement over whether the concept of "body" in wine involves alcohol alone or alcohol and extract. Arguing the point does no good. The way to assess the effect of different levels of alcohol is to *taste* simultaneously several wines of the same type which have different levels of alcohol. A little sleuthing plus assistance from a knowledgeable wine merchant will help here. An interesting point of comparison might be two contrasting Zinfandels, one from the cooler (lighter bodied) 1972 vintage, and the other of the same maker from the warmer (fuller bodied) 1971 vintage.

Taking Zinfandel as an example, a red wine made from Zinfandel grapes picked at 22° sugar (=11% alcohol) will be light, perhaps austere, but not necessarily lacking in depth of flavor. At 24° sugar (=12–12.5%

alcohol) the wine will be fuller, perhaps fruitier. At 26° sugar (= 13–14% alcohol) the wine will be rich and slightly heady, reminiscent, perhaps, of a fine Hermitage from the Rhône Valley, France. It might also be interesting to taste a lineup of Johannisberg Rieslings ranging from a Moselle at 10.5% alcohol to a Napa Johannisberg Riesling at 14% alcohol.

We have already discussed several bases of flavor in wine. Extract (non-sugar soluble solids) seems to be progressively higher as alcohol increases. It is difficult to understand *why* this is so. Complex *interrelationships* of chemical elements are difficult to assess; it is even more difficult to understand how all these elements interact on the palate. Is it possible that progressively higher sugar to water ratios in the grape juice has a progressively greater capacity to absorb certain types of extract? And does acidity play a significant role? Energy forms such as sugar and alcohol seem to be particularly suited to absorb and suspend extract. Glycerol is considered by some oenologists to be particularly important for giving a foundation to flavor and body in wine.

The higher the alcohol, it seems, the *heavier* the extract, the more "full-bodied" is the wine. Extract derived from the effect of high sugar and alcohol seems to differ somewhat from extract derived from other viticultural factors: careful pruning, the age of the vines, water supply, soil makeup, etc. A comparison of a 10.5% alcohol Moselle Riesling of superior quality with a Freemark Abbey Johannisberg Riesling (Napa) at 13.5% alcohol might illustrate the difference. The Moselle will be intensely flavored; first because of its delicate sugar/acid balance, and second because the very limited productivity of hillside vineyards along the Moselle tends to intensify extract content. The Napa Riesling is deeply flavored more as a result of its *body*. The concept of body in sensory analysis is (and perhaps should be) somewhat vague. Extensive comparisons will clarify it.

It is important to understand the difference between the two basic quality factors, flavor and body. Heavily cropped grapes from vineyards in very warm climate will often be lacking in flavor intensity although they might have excellent *body* derived from high levels of sugar in the grapes and alcohol in the wines. It is not unusual for less scrupulous wine producers in California to misrepresent their products by claiming that the full-bodied character of their wine is the result of severe pruning to produce a low-yield harvest.

Once the winemaker has decided when to pick the grapes, it is important to the quality of the wine that the grapes are picked quickly and carefully and delivered to the winery as soon as possible—certainly on the same day that they are picked. Small estates such as Mayacamas or Chalone in California and small Chateaux in the Bordeaux region have a major advantage in this respect. The grapes can be picked at the instant they reach the perfection of ripeness and delivered to the winery within a very short time.

The actual stemming and crushing of the fruit is a fairly simple matter, thanks to modern, efficient equipment. Most California wineries are on an equal footing in this respect because most modern stemming-crushing equipment is of the same basic design. Differences are mostly in terms of size and capacity. There are still a few smaller wineries, however, which use old-fashioned stemmer-crushers. The white wines especially will often have a curiously coarse and off-tasting "stemmy" character.

The process of *fermentation* is absolutely crucial. The care with which the grapes are fermented is immediately reflected in the quality of the wine. We are not concerned, here, so much with the chemistry of fermentation as we are with understanding the options open to the winemaker during the fermentation process and the way in which different choices among those options affect the quality and style of the wine; i.e., the artistic/aesthetic considerations.

The fermentation process is at once extremely complex and transparently simple: complex from the point of view of the wine chemist who studies the actual organic process which occurs; and simple in that the basic definition of the process is simple; i.e., the natural sugars in the grape juices are transformed, through the action of yeast, into alcohol while two by-products (heat and carbon dioxide) are given off.

In the fermentation of white wine, the juice is first allowed to run off through a screen from the seeds and crushed skins. Additional juice is then obtained by pressing out the skins. There is a widely held belief in California that the best white wine is made from the first, "free run," juice. The pressed juice is generally kept separate and fermented separately being considered coarser and of lower quality than "free run" juice. This is a cherished California myth which is certainly not necessarily true. Most European winemakers would laugh at this belief. Generally, it is the juice from the first light pressing which gives body and character to the wine, and is the more highly flavored.

The juice of white wine grapes does not look like the clean, clear liquid which is the end product, the wine. It is a rather murky looking liquid containing a great many natural impurities. Many winemakers who are developing a clean, limpid style in their white wine, will allow the juice to settle in large tanks for anywhere from twelve to twenty four hours, so that some of the denser impurities have a chance to settle out. The must is then drawn off these "lees" into another tank and then innoculated with the yeast which initiates the fermentation.

The juice of white wine grapes is particularly fragile and susceptible to a whole range of "ills" if it is not handled with exceptional care. Sulfur dioxide has become a kind of panacea for a good many of those problems and if used judiciously will prevent a multitude of problems. Excessive sulfur will show up as a very disagreeable odor in the wine.

Oxygen is the worst enemy of white winemaking especially during these first stages. Preventing any but the most minute contact of oxygen with the must and the wine as it develops during fermentation taxes the ingenuity of the winemaker and the efficiency of his equipment which may range from a simple valve which lets out carbon dioxide and prevents oxygen from entering the closed container, to an elaborate, pressurized stainless steel or glass lined tank.

The initial stages of red wine fermentation are considerably different. Here the crushed and stemmed berries (juice, skins and seeds) all go directly to the fermentation vats, along with a suitable amount of sulfur to sterilize the must. Although there are natural strains of yeast which attach themselves to the exterior of all fruit, California winemakers almost universally use special, pure yeast strains which are more efficient and work at more desirable rates of speed. Most of these are derived from yeast cultures which are indigenous to certain European vineyards. This use of pure strains does not make the wine any less "natural". They are a significant quality factor tending to give superior results.

The major difference in red wine fermentation is the fact that it need not take place in anaerobic conditions; i.e., contact of the fermenting must with oxygen is not harmful. It is important, perhaps, to understand why.

All fruit, being a part of the reproductive system of plants, is essentially a fertilized seed. In its natural function, the fruit falls to the soil, and its flesh disintegrates naturally under the action of natural yeasts, bacteria, and oxygen, providing moisture and fertilizer to the soil which will support the growth of the seed. The seed is provided with a coating of tough fibrous material which will protect it from the immediate deteriorating effects of oxygen but is sufficient to protect it from the elements only through the winter. One of the natural, relatively stable components of this protective fiber is a form of acid known as tannin. Tannin forms a protective resistence to the deteriorating action of oxygen, providing this protection not only to the seed, but to the stems, trunk and branches or vines as well. There is even tannin in the skin of the fruit to help it in *its* protective capacity. The protection which tannin provides is not complete, however, since the seed casing eventually disintegrates, and trunk and branches must renew themselves every year with a new layer of protective bark.

Tannin acts in a similar but stronger anti-oxidant capacity than most other acids. Examples of the anti-oxidant capacities of other acids would be the pickling, preservative capacity of acetic acid (vinegar). Cooks will think of the anti-oxidant properties of citric acid (lemon juice) in keeping cut artichokes or apples from turning brown or keeping sautéed mushrooms white.

In the initial stages of red wine fermentation, there is sufficient tannin in the skins to provide immediate protection from oxygen. As the fermentation proceeds, additional tannin is leeched out of the seeds and becomes incorporated into the juices. The pure juice of most red wine grapes is not in fact red, but is anywhere from colorless to faint pink. There are only a few varieties (Alicante Bouchet, Salvador, Rubired, Royalty) which have juice which is decidedly red. As the fermentation proceeds, however, both tannin and the red pigment which is located in the skins become incorporated into the juice, making it at first faint pink, then rose colored (after about five hours), to light red and finally deep purple, depending on how long the juice remains in contact with the skins. In California, the Zinfandel grape is used to make a "white" wine (a wine made from juice which has had no contact with the crushed skins); a pink or rosé wine (wine fermented on the skins for about eight hours); and a full-fledged red wine (wine left in contact with the skins for several days). A side by side taste comparison of all three would be very interesting and highly instructive.

As the fermentation becomes active, the skins and seeds become separated from the juice, floating to the top and forming what is known as the "cap". This cap is re-incorporated into the juice at certain intervals by pumping juice from the bottom of the tank and pouring it out over the cap, or else by "punching down" the cap into the juice by means of paddles.

In addition to color and tannin, and perhaps most important of all, major flavor constituents are extracted from the skins and other cellular constituents of the berry in this process. A great deal of winemaking theory and practice in California has grossly oversimplified this crucial stage. The very common, blanket assumption is made that the sole purpose of fermentation of wine on the skins and seeds is to extract tannin from the seeds and skins and pigment from the skins; and that the process should take only as long as the desired color is absorbed into the juice (one to three days). While this may be true for strictly commercial grade wines, it hardly applies to fine wines made from premium grape varieties.

Up to a certain point (perhaps eight to twelve days), the longer red wine ferments on the skins, the more color, the more tannin and the more flavor constituents will be extracted from the cap, provided of course, that the grapes are of excellent quality and the fermentation is well managed. The winemaker's decision should be predicated on the quality and the potential of the grapes. Certainly it would be a waste to give overcropped, poorly balanced grapes a lengthy fermentation on the skins. By the time the tannin softened with years of bottle age, there would probably be nothing left to the wine.

On the other hand, it would be a minor tragedy if grapes of exceptional quality and potential were given a very brief fermentation on the skins. I have had the opportunity to taste two red wines made from the same lot of grapes, one was made at a commercial winery by leaving the wine on the skins for eighteen hours until the wine was sufficiently colored to be able to call it a red wine. The other was a small lot of wine made by the grower himself. This second wine was left on the skins for twelve days and the cap was punched down at regular intervals. The first wine was attractive enough, rather light and at its full potential only three years after the vintage, a rather slick luncheon type wine. The second was a huge, dark, elegant wine with masses of fruit, just beginning to show its full potential at three years old.

Premium winemaking practice in Europe, especially in the finer Chateaux of the Bordeaux region and in the finer domaines of Burgundy, has traditionally let the finest wines ferment on the skins for periods of approximately twelve days. At Chateau Latour, however, the wine ferments on the skins for a considerably longer period. Europeans who visit the California winemaking scene are continually amazed that the wines are fermented on the skins for so short a time. There are major exceptions, however: the Cabernets of Mayacamas, Ridge, and some older Krug Cabernets are made in the European manner. Those who have the patience to let these wines age out to their potential will be amply rewarded.

There is a problem with red wine which many California wine producers have approached in a rather ostrich-like manner. Fermenting red wine on the skins produces color *and* tannin *and* important flavor constituents. Unfortunately, the more flavor that is extracted, the more tannin is extracted. Tannin is a very disagreeable aspect of young red wine, attacking the palate as it does, giving the wine an almost sand-paper texture. With age the tannin softens; it combines with pigments and other impurities in the wine to form solid particles which precipitate out of the wine as sediment. One of the precious by-products of this process, however, is richness and complexity of bouquet and flavor.

In a situation where wine producers are trying to build a broad based market, they have to accomodate the immediate likes and dislikes of the novice wine drinker. The novice not only finds tannin disagreeable (as well he might), but it is virtually impossible to tell him to put his wine away for a few years. Wine producers in California have done everything in their power to let the consumer have his cake and eat it too. Some have been trying to produce a high quality red wine which has full flavor and finesse without tannin, without sediment, and without the need for further aging. All kinds of cellar treatment has been devised to get around the basic fact of life of fine red wine. No matter how the winemakers try to get the tannin back out of red wine, the flavor seems to go out right along with it.

There is no question that tannin and sediment are a nuisance, particularly if one buys all wines on a day to day basis for immediate consumption. Wine which has thrown a sediment has to be handled carefully so that the precipitate is not shaken up with the wine, often making it cloudy. Many consumers simply do not want to be bothered. Often it is the housewife who complains, thinking that the wine is defective or unclean. And it is not just the American who complains; wine merchants in Europe have the same problems with people who complain about sediment.

The wine and spirits distributors upon whom most commercial wineries depend also want a strictly clean, ready-made product. The distributor could not care less about educating the wine buying public, and God knows he does not want to be bothered by complaints about sediment. He wants a product which is as easy to sell as beer and whiskey. Furthermore, why bother to educate clerks and the wine buying public when clever packaging and hard-sell advertising will move merchandise just as well?

There is simply no way around the situation. Both red and white premium quality wines are not ready-made products. Red wines and even some white wines of any distinction will be tannic and disagreeable when they are young and will throw a deposit as they develop bottle age. Cellaring wines either in one's own home cellar or in an accomodating merchant's cellar, is an absolute necessity for those who want the full aesthetic enjoyment which premium quality wine can give.

Decanting an aged wine off its sediment is really the simplest thing in the world to do. The less fuss made over it, the better. All that is needed is some source of light which will shine through from below the bottle; a lamp, a candle, often a white table cloth will be sufficient. One simply pours the wine out carefully into a decanter and as the dark arrow of sediment reaches the neck of the bottle, one stops pouring. Elementary!

Granted, one loses an ounce or two of wine, but consider the alternative: highly processed, sterile wine which will never have the quality potential of the wine which quite naturally throws a sediment.[1]

Besides the extraction of tannin, pigment and flavor which occurs in fermentation, there is another important factor which occurs as a by product of fermentation; namely, heat. The degree of heat which is generated by fermentation has an effect on the pace at which the fermentation proceeds. The manner in which this general pacing is managed is a very important quality factor. Generally, the warmer the fermentation, the faster will it accomplish its work—but only up to a point. A fermentation which gets too warm will destroy the efficacy of the yeast. Such a fermentation is called"stuck". Like a Hollandaise sauce that curdles, it is impossible to "un-stick" (or un-curdle) it on its own—it has to be added to another fermenting must.

There is no prescribed, absolute temperature for fermentation. It should be predicated on the makeup of each particular must, depending upon the type of grape, where it is grown, the sugar/acid balance, and the style which the winemaker is developing. It is largely an artistic judgment. Cooler fermentation temperatures are generally maintained in fermenting California white wines. Because of their generally lower acidity, every effort has to be made to maintain and preserve whatever acids exist in order to balance the wine. The lower temperature is often controlled by refrig-

---

[1] One of the most interesting discussions on the art of decanting is contained in the superb chapter "How to Drink Wine" which Arpad Haraszthy wrote for Frona Eunice Wait's book, *Wines and Vines of California* (1889). Reprinted by Howell-North Books, Berkeley, California; 1973.

eration coils which encircle stainless steel fermentation vats. One less fortunate winemaker had to rig up a fan which blew onto cakes of ice which were set near his fermentation casks. It turned out to be one of those cases of "who has the last laugh now"—his white wines made international news for their exceptional quality only two years later. Slow, cool (but not cold) fermentation of white wine tends not to distort the delicate fruit extracts so that the wines are more reflective of the character of the grape. A slower, more orderly fermentation seems to aid in the production of esters and higher alcohols which are necessary for bouquet.

In Italy, the south of France, Australia, Russia and California, there has been considerable experimentation with heat-treated red wine musts as a means of extracting greater pigment and less tannin for bulk type wines. This method has come to be known as the "thermo-vascular" method and is being further developed in California at Gallo and at the Souverain of Alexander Valley winery north of Healdsburg.

For red wine made in the classical manner, many winemakers prefer a steady, unrelenting, very even fermentation in the 70°–75° range. There seems to be a correlation in the culinary preparation of fine meat stocks and sauces, for which a steady, unrelenting simmer develops the richest, most finely textured results. Other winemakers (Parducci, for example) will let the temperature go up to 90° for a short period of time, believing that this process gives the wine some additional character. The consumer should understand that a slow, patient fermentation ties up expensive winemaking equipment during the critical time of harvest. With a quick fermentation, a far greater quantity of wine can be produced, with greater return on the investment which the producer has in his equipment.

It is almost inevitably more costly to breed significant quality factors into finer wine. The consumer should expect to pay more. Again, each lover of fine wine should reflect very carefully on his own scale of wine values and understand the additional cost factors which are necessary to produce them.

Following the completion of the fermentation, there need not be much further processing of the wine, again an artistic decision on the part of the winemaker. More often than not, the decision in favor of further, even excessive, processing is a matter of commercial necessity rather than an aesthetic judgment. At this point there are two basic occurrences. In the first of these, the winemaker simply lets the impurities in the wine (dead yeast cells, bits of skin, traces of soil, etc.) settle to the bottom, at which time the wine is drawn off these "dregs" in the operation called "racking".[1] Usually several rackings are necessary before the wine is bottled. The second is the normal, but not necessarily universal, occurrence of what is termed the "malo-lactic fermentation". It is simply a transformation of the slightly fiercer malic acid into the softer, less assertive lactic acid by means of lactic acid bacteria. It seems that the overall quality of the wine improves as a result. It is termed a fermentation because there is a by-product of carbon dioxide; malo-lactic fermentation which is not complete when the wine is bottled will complete itself in the bottle, causing a slight effervescence due to the residual carbon dioxide.

There are other finishing processes which the wine might undergo at the discretion of the winemaker, namely fining and filtering. These are mostly intended to affect the appearance of the wine, to give brilliance and clarity. There is a danger (and this is a controversial matter) that either or both of these processes might also remove important flavor constituents.

Filtering is more or less self-explanatory, although there are wide variations among filters in their ability to selectively filter out particles which are deleterious while leaving those which enhance the wine. Robert Mondavi winery has often released both filtered and unfiltered versions of the same wine—comparing them is a revelation! It is important to note that filtering is by no means *necessary*, as any impurities will eventually settle out

---

[1] If the first racking is not done *immediately* following the completion of the fermentation, all kinds of problems and disagreeable flavors and odors will develop in the wine.

of the wine quite naturally. Sediment can be a nuisance, though. If one buys all wine from the corner liquor store for immediate consumption, then sediment is indeed a nuisance. Such a casual, random wine buyer probably could not detect any difference which heavy filtering might make in a wine; but a discriminating, reflective wine drinker certainly should be able to detect the difference. This is why a small backlog of wine in the form of a wine cellar is virtually a necessity for the discriminating wine drinker.[1] A very good case could be made to support the thesis that the practice of over-filtering is one of the greatest stumbling blocks to the emergence of the potential greatness of California premium wines.

Fining is the process by which a proteinaceous substance such as egg white or gelatin is added to the wine at the top. As the protein settles it carries along with it any tiny suspended particles which might tend to make the wine cloudy or less than brilliantly clear. Most California wines go through at least a light fining although one will occasionally run across a wine marked "unfined".[2] Anyone interested in quality wines should make side by side comparisons of fined and unfined wines in order to understand the quality differences involved.

The culinary process which cooks call "clarifying the meat stock for consommé" is essentially the same. For a second-hand understanding of fining, try clarifying a good meat stock with egg white, according to any number of classic recipes. Notice the appearance before and after, but also take note of the flavor before and after. A successful stock clarification will render the stock a brilliant, clear amber color. The stock may not be as full bodied, but it will have a cleaner, more elegant flavor. Here, one bases one's

---

[1] By this I do not mean to deny that there is an important place for intermediate, commercial grade wines which are bought on a day to day basis.

[2] For example, some of the wines of Parducci (Ukiah).

preference, not on any absolute rule, but on the intended style and use of the stock (or the wine). In the case of the meat stock, one might want a brilliant, lustrous amber consommé to precede Tournedos Rossini in an elegant dinner. If the stock were to precede, say, charcoal broiled, thick cut, filet steaks, one would perhaps be willing to sacrifice a brilliant appearance for a more hearty, full-bodied broth, garnished with a julienne of vegetables. With the Tournedos, one would perhaps prefer a brilliant, carefully but lightly fined Claret (most of the finest Medocs are lightly fined). But with the charcoal broiled steaks, perhaps one would prefer a dark, full-bodied, unfined California Zinfandel.

One final note on filtering and fining. Many California wine "judges" who use a rigid, mathematical judging scheme, assign a very important place to the clarity of wine—where clarity is taken as a completely negative value—meaning lack of visible suspended particles. What this has done, perhaps, is to encourage many winemakers to over fine and over filter their wines to the point of sterility, sacrificing complexity and nuance of flavor to satisfy the predilection which many people have for very clean looking wines. Commercial necessity reinforces this desire for very clean, highly filtered and fined wines.

The aesthetic appeal of the appearance of really fine wine is not so much clarity as it is luminosity—the touchstone of all exceptionally fine wine. Very difficult to describe or define, luminosity is rather like the difference between cut diamond and cut glass. It involves the depth and intensity of the appropriate color of the wine. It seems to indicate a density of fruit extract which contributes to richness of flavor. Glycerol, too, seems to contribute luster to fine wine as well as provide an excellent foundation for rich flavor. Perfectly clear, clean wines never offend, but richly luminous, lustrous wines generate excitement and the anticipation of special quality. The aesthetic character of the appearance of wine cannot be assessed in abstraction from bouquet and taste. One should assess the appearance of a wine by the way it contributes a cohesive rhythm to the aesthetic enjoyment of wine.

Perhaps the most important finishing process, and certainly the most elusive in terms of the quality factor which it contributes, is *wood aging*, normally done in cooperage made of oak. Writers have long avoided comment on the effects which aging in oak or other types of wood has on a wine, arguing obscurity and the difficulty of pinning down the flavor contributions of wood (to say nothing about describing these flavors with words.)

One of the benefits of the experimental attitude of some California winemakers is that we have come closer than ever in our ability to understand the aesthetic contribution of cooperage. Winemakers have made extensive comparative studies of the effect which different cooperage has on the same wine. They have put wines, traditionally aged in a certain type of casks, into different types of casks or perhaps in no wood at all. All this cross comparison has given us the point of view necessary to develop a clearer perception of the flavors and aromas which cooperage contributes to wine. The general conclusion is that cooperage contributes a great deal more to the general quality and character of wine than was ever suspected.

These are not occult flavor nuances which only the most sophisticated palate can detect. Even with a modest amount of carefully chosen comparative tasting, one will be able to isolate these different flavors and understand the contribution which cooperage makes to the general quality of the wine.

Because fine cooperage for aging wine has jumped from a minor to a major cost factor in only a few short years, it is important to understand how fine cooperage enhances the quality of wine, particularly with a view to making judgments of value for money in wine.

Barrel aging has two basic functions. Oak and other barrel woods have a certain porosity which admits small amounts of oxygen. The principle is similar to that of the cork in the bottle which allows a very gradual oxydation of the wine, but not enough to overwhelm or spoil the wine. This gradual oxydation of the wine, both through the cork in the bottle and through the wood of the barrel, softens the tannin, allows impurities to settle out of the wine, and contributes to the development of aroma and bouquet in the wine. The porosity of the *barrel* also releases a certain percentage of the wine itself through evaporation. During a two year residence in an oak barrel, there is roughly a five percent loss of the original volume (not including loss due to precipitation of sediment). This loss must be made up at regular intervals (a process called "topping up") in order to protect the wine from a too rapid oxydation. This task demands special care and discipline on the part of the winemaker. Anything less will have an adverse affect on the wines.

In the second basic function of barrel aging, the slow interchange of oxygen and wine through the pores of the wood has a unique effect. The wine absorbs very distinct flavors, odors and tannins from the wood. White wines and brandies which are aged in oak also extract a certain amount of pigment from the wood. Spirits distilled from wine are colorless. Ordinary brandy is generally colored by the use of caramel, but Cognacs and fine brandies derive their amber hue from oak.

Different woods vary considerably in both porosity and in the flavors, perfumes and tannins which they contribute to the wines they hold. Oak is perhaps the best wood for cooperage because it combines general sturdiness with suitable porosity, and in some instances very desirable odor-flavor constituents. Redwood, chestnut and locust are other cooperage woods which have various advantages and disadvantages.

Among the different types of oak cooperage used in making California premium wine, there are three types which predominate: Limousin oak (from forests near the city of Limoges, France), Nevers oak (from forests near the city of Nevers, France) and White American oak (from the Ozark Mountains).

Of the three types of oak, Limousin gives the wine the most delicate flavor and aroma and the least amount of tannin; and is, therefore, considered the most suitable for white wine and the more delicate, subtler reds. In France, Limousin is used in making fine white and red Burgundy and for making the finest Cognacs. The distinct "vanilla" aroma of Cognac, as well as the delicate, nutty mellowness of White Burgundy and some California Chardonnays which resemble them, derive from Limousin. Depending upon the type of wine put into the barrel, on cellar conditions and length of time in the barrel, Limousin can impart quite remarkable nuances of flavor, particularly with bottle age. The oak flavor can be quite predominant when the wine is young, but as it develops bottle age, the flavor can recede into the background and develop intriguing new aroma-flavor characteristics. The dark, cocoa/coffee-bean bouquet of some older French Red Burgundies probably derives from just such a mingling of fruit and oak as it develops in the bottle.

Nevers oak is somewhat more powerful in its flavor effect than Limousin oak. This is the cooperage used primarily for fine Bordeaux wines. The aromas and flavors of Nevers oak are more distinctly "oak" aromas, sharing more of the character of the raw wood. It has a way of enhancing the black currant character of fine Cabernet Sauvignon and the raspberry character of Zinfandel. Some of the bigger California Chardonnays are put into Nevers oak for a few months to take on the rich character of that oak, quite distinct from Chardonnay which is aged in Limousin. An interesting comparison tasting might include a Cardonnay of Freemark Abbey (Nevers oak), a Chardonnay or Pinot Blanc of Chalone Vineyards (Limousin oak), and the Chardonnay of Hacienda Vineyards (Sonoma) or Wente Brothers (both made with no wood at all).

White American oak imparts by far the most pungent raw oak character. This is the oak which gives its characteristic aroma to Bourbon whiskey. A very fine eight year old California brandy from Royal Host Cellars of Lodi has an intriguing aroma of American oak which makes it more reminiscent of fine Bourbon than of the vanilla/Limousin character of

Cognac. Special care has to be exercised in putting wine into American oak because the oak flavors and tannin can throw the wine off balance. Dr. David Bruce has made brilliant use of American oak by putting it around some highly alcoholic, racy wines from late harvest grapes, notably Zinfandel and Black Muscat. The very individual wines of Leo Trentadue (Alexander Valley) are particularly pungent with the flavors of American oak.

Large redwood vats are also used in California. Redwood is supposed to be a neutral wood, imparting very little wood character, but this is nonsense. Only a proper point of comparison is necessary to detect the rich, somewhat resinous character which redwood imparts to wine. Redwood "chips" are sold on the west coast as a garden mulch; take a good sniff of some of these wood chips to get some idea of the redwood aroma. Used judiciously, redwood can greatly enhance the characteristic fruitiness of California red wine at a fraction of the cost of French oak cooperage. A revealing taste comparison would be the Sebastiani Gamay Beaujolais Nouveau (no wood) against their regular Gamay Beaujolais (aged in redwood tanks).

Many premium quality wines from California will state on the back label exactly what kind of cooperage was used and for how long. By making careful, side by side comparisons it is not difficult to develop some fairly accurate idea of the flavors and aromatic characteristics of different types of wood.

In the foregoing discussion of viticulture and winemaking, I have emphasized aspects which most directly concern the person who buys and enjoys wines of special quality. I have passed over a great many problems which pertain to the specific business of the grower and winemaker: for example, problems and techniques of propagating the vines, controlling pests and disease, pruning, testing and chemical analysis, managing the many special problems which arise in both the basic fermentation and the malo-lactic fermentation, etc. There has been a vast amount of scientific intelligence applied to these problems, especially in California. Perhaps more than any other wine region, California produces the highest percentage of wines which are, *at the very least*, sound, palatable and free from major disorders.

All of the various aspects of viticulture and winemaking which I have discussed, in addition to these other more technical aspects, are crucially important, each in their own way. It is most important, however, for the winemaker to orchestrate all of these means in order to produce the best wine possible—to achieve a successful balance of interrelationships between all these factors. These interrelationships cannot be reduced to a mechanical or scientific formula. Premium winemaking is a very complex art form.

The achievement of balance and style demands years of experience. A winemaker needs to watch many of his wines through their brief or lengthy histories; perceiving, for example, the result in 1976 of something which was done in 1972. Balance is achieved by managing and disposing all the various factors with a certain sense of economy. Only the finest wine should go into the best new barrels; only the very best grapes undergo the lengthiest fermentation on the skins; only appropriate and complementary wines are blended together, each balancing deficiencies in the other, so that the marriage is superior to any of the elements taken alone. Complexity in wine derives not only from the quality of the grapes but even more from a delicate balance of elements achieved by the winemaker's art. This demands a great deal of intelligence, good taste, dedication and tenacity. The scientific frame of mind recedes in importance, becoming one of several means to an end; taste, aesthetic judgment and experience become the ultimate guides.

The perception of this balance of elements is at the very heart of aesthetic enjoyment and appreciation of fine wine. These balanced inter-relationships are not well defined, fixed, external and measurable. We enjoy our wine, not in the laboratory, but as part of the pleasure of the table. Reducing these interrelationships to mathematical ratios, scoring and point summation will not help our aesthetic enjoyment. Style, balance and finesse are artistic achievements. We perceive these values in wine in the same way that we perceive them in any other art form.

As wine is not a static entity, neither is perception a static event. Both are organic processes in time. Aesthetic perception focuses now on one aspect; now on another special quality, taking note how the wine comes to life in the glass, making comparisons with other wines in memory and, perhaps, the same wine as it tasted a year ago. Perhaps a scent in the wine calls forth an awareness of a kindred scent imbedded in the fringe of memory. There is a rhythm to our enjoyment. The experienced wine lover has learned to concentrate and make a synthesis of his perceptions of various qualities and his reminiscences. The broader his experience, the richer and more fecund will be his overall response to the wine. The cultivation of a good wine memory is one of the keys to this higher level of wine appreciation.

There are interesting similarities between wine and music. Fine wine develops in the bottle in a way that is similar to thematic development in serious music. The basic themes undergo transformations through which they develop depth and complexity of interrelation. Effects which are well organized become cumulative and climactic. The enjoyment of music and the enjoyment of wine are also similar. Both require a well-developed memory and the ability to synthesize the various stages of development. The experienced wine lover is always interested in the history of a well-made wine.

There is really no absolute "peak" in the development of a wine. As we do not necessarily enjoy a musical climax the most, there is no point in the life of a wine at which we will necessarily enjoy it the most. As the best wines are developing, there are shifts of emphasis in the overall balance. There is a stage during which the wine seems to be most completely realized, but one also enjoys a young wine's precociousness, the way it has been constructed to have a potential for future excellence; older wine can be loved for its soundness and complexity in spite of the grey hairs. Fine wines also change in the way that they function at the table. Young and fresh, a white wine might be lovely with trout; older and fuller, the same wine might want a fine Poulet à la Crème. Many of the basic, classic wines of California—for example certain vintages of Beaulieu Private Reserve Cabernet Sauvignon, some Louis Martini Zinfandels, Spring Mountain Chardonnay, Wente Brothers Sauvignon Blanc—have the characteristic of being perfectly useful in different ways throughout their richly developing careers.

Music is perhaps more sophisticated and complex than the visual arts, touching a more profound layer of the human psyche; perceiving and understanding wine as a developing process is also the more complex and sophisticated aspect of wine appreciation and a source of some of its keenest pleasures.

The California Scene—

The Environment

Five

There is a mystique about the name "California". In many languages it has developed the connotation of a kind of new "promised land"—magnificent mountains, broad fertile valleys, sunshine in abundance, fruits ripening in lush orchards. How remarkably the reality measures up to the mystique, particularly in wine country California! Certainly it is one of the loveliest vine growing regions of the world.

Except for the Bordelais, perhaps no vine growing region has as sophisticated a city at its center as San Francisco. Somehow very European in style, San Francisco is committed to the arts, to good living and the enjoyment of good food and wine. The pace of life is relaxed and friendly, with less of the commercial heaviness one finds in so many American cities; and like New York and New Orleans, it takes its gastronomy very seriously. In 1875, Dumas wrote in the *Dictionary of Cuisine* that, after Paris, the city with the most restaurants is San Francisco. This is no longer true, but the tradition of gastronomy is very much alive—with a whole galaxy of fine restaurants representing all of the great cuisines of the world.

From any one of the several steep hills of San Francisco there is a spectacular view of San Francisco Bay, which stretches north and south for many miles—the tentacles of the bay reaching out toward the great California vineyards. The bay is almost completely land bound, being fed through the Golden Gate, a five-mile-wide break in a narrow chain of coastal mountains which rise abruptly and dramatically from the Pacific. Inland, the Sonoma, Napa, Livermore and Santa Clara Valleys fan out from the bay, each on a line which points toward San Francisco and the Golden Gate. These are the fine grape growing and winemaking valleys of California. Several miles farther inland lies the broad, hot, fertile Sacramento Valley and its southern extension, the San Joaquin Valley. Combined, there are over ten thousand square miles of lush farm land, a giant fruit and vegetable bowl. And then beyond, lie the magnificent "High Sierras".

During the summer, temperatures in Sacramento range between 80° and 110° Farenheit, while 75 miles west in San Francisco temperatures will be a cool 65°, falling to 55° in the evening. The hot, rising air of the vast interior valley attracts masses of cool ocean air. The coastal mountains form a barrier so that most of the ocean breezes are funneled through the Golden Gate, across the city and the bay and along the grapegrowing valleys which act as cool air corridors: a kind of giant, natural air-conditioning system. These ocean breezes are more like rivers of sea air, so well defined that at certain points one can virtually walk in and out of them and feel the difference. In the vineyard valleys, throughout the morning, the air is relatively still, the sun is bright and warm. As temperatures rise, the air begins to stir. By early afternoon, gentle zephyrs temper the heat. While the citrus and olive groves and nut orchards of the great interior valley are flourishing and enjoying the 100° heat, the vineyard valleys are enjoying a normal 75° to 85° temperature. The breezes keep the atmosphere comfortable and invigorating. In San Francisco, strollers in Golden Gate Park wear sweaters in the cool 63° afternoon temperature. Mark Twain once remarked that the coldest winter he had ever experienced was a summer in San Francisco! Even more remarkable is the fact that San Francisco is located on the same degree latitude as Sicily and the northern tip of Mediterranean Africa.

There is a visible phenomenon which shows quite graphically how this great "aero-dynamic" system works. On a good many summer mornings one can see a great mass of fog lurking several miles off the Golden Gate. By early afternoon, as the rising hot air mass of the central valley draws in the cool ocean air, the fog mass is carried along at somewhat less than the speed of an ocean liner. A giant arrow of fog hurtles directly toward the Golden Gate. Although there are a few other breaks in the coastal range, the Golden Gate is the largest and most important. By 3:00

p.m., the fog mass is pouring through the gate, eclipsing all but the towers of the Golden Gate Bridge, and fanning out over the bay in the directions of the wine districts.

The effect of this vast aero-dynamic system is to create a complex, incredibly varied system of micro-climates in and around the San Francisco Bay Area. Wherever in the world grapes are grown to make fine wine, there is a climate in some area of California vineyards to match.

Taking cognizance of this system, the oenologists at the University of California/Davis in the late 1930's mapped out this micro-climatic system, breaking it down into five basic types of grape growing regions. They used the principle of heat summation which works as follows. Recognizing the fact that grape vines make no appreciable growth in temperatures less than 50°, the university measured the daily mean temperature at sample points throughout the wine country and made recordings for every day throughout the growing season. The same type of temperature data was collected in the great grapevine growing regions of Europe. The daily mean temperature in excess of the 50° was called the "degree day" and the total of these heat units throughout the growing season was called the "heat summation". Region I was delimited to vineyard areas with a heat summation of 2500 or less. Examples of region I were found to be the Rhine and Moselle districts of Germany, Champagne in France, much of Switzerland, and areas near the towns of Napa, Santa Cruz and Santa Rosa in California. Region II, still fairly cool, has a heat summation of 2501–3000 and would characterize the middle of the Napa Valley, the Sonoma Valley, and the Santa Clara Valley of California and the region near the city of Bordeaux, France. Region III, 3001–3500, is typical of the northern Napa Valley and Livermore in California and Tuscany in Italy. Region IV, 3501–4000, characterizes areas near the California towns of Ukiah, Davis, Lodi and Cucamonga, and much of Sicily, Greece and central Spain. Region V is the hottest, 4001 or more, and includes the majority of the Sacramento and San Joaquin Valleys of California, as well as vineyard areas of Morocco, Algeria and southern Spain.

The aero-dynamic system which governs the California grape growing regions creates a very stable high-pressure system over the region during the late spring, summer and early fall, making the area not only rain-proof, but practically cloudless throughout the growing season. Not only are the temperatures of these regions similar to the great European vineyard areas, but the general climate is comparable to these regions when they are experiencing a rare, weather-perfect year! During the late fall, winter and early spring, a low pressure system comes in from the northwest and anchors off the coast, bringing steady soaking rains—chilling, but seldom freezing. Every decade or so, San Francisco has a snow fall which lasts a day or two at most.

Each year, spring weather brings a very real danger. As the winter rain system is gradually supplanted by the summer cloud-free weather, a succession of warm spring days can encourage early budding in the vineyards. Along the coast, the proximity to masses of water maintains nightime temperatures above the freezing level. Inland, a nightime cloud or fog cover helps keep temperatures above freezing. But without this cover, there is an extreme danger of nightime frosts killing off the early flowering of the vines. Driving through the Napa Valley, huge propellers, mounted atop steel towers can be seen, curious sentinels of the vineyards. At the least warning of spring frost, these propellers are driven to keep air circulating and reduce the chances that freezing air will settle in among the vines. In the vineyards which produce the costlier crops, a new system of tiny jet-spray sprinklers is used—the moisture from the sprinklers freezes on contact with the vines and forms a wafer-thin shield of ice which maintains the temperature at 32° but not below.

Driving toward Napa on Highway 121 at the point where one loses sight of the bay, there is a series of gently rolling hills which form a kind of apron to the entrance of the Napa Valley. Here, the abrupt ending of the two mountain ranges which define the valley can be seen ahead and to the left. Vineyards appear here and there among the rolling hills—marking the beginning of the Carneros district of the valley. The plantings are relatively recent, mostly under the direction of Beaulieu's Andre Tchelistcheff who sought cool, region I vineyard land for his Pinot Noir, Chardonnay and Johannisberg Riesling. Other plantings go to make the wines of the Sonoma based Z-D Winery, among others.

The valley itself, like a huge curving blade of a Turkish sword, lies between the Mayacamas Mountain Range to the west and the Howell Mountain Range to the east, tapering to a point which lies at the foot of Mount St. Helena. The area was originally part of an ocean bed. The valley floor, as it exists today, is quite level at most points and was most likely the creation of tremendous lava flows from some of the surrounding mountains. The tips of some prehistoric hills which were almost totally buried by the flow, jut abruptly up and out of the valley floor, at points south of the town of Yountville and, at the northern end, a few miles north of the town of St. Helena. The hot springs and geysers near the town of Calistoga are mementos of this prehistoric volcanic activity.

Although there is an occasional outcropping of red clay soils, and, along the part of the valley floor which is up close to the Mayacamas Range, occasional gravelly alluvial deposits made by streams which once descended from the mountains, the soil base in the Napa Valley is volcanic ash and lava debris. This crumbly, porous soil provides the same sort of good drainage which one finds in the sand/gravel soil complex of the Bordeaux region. Roughly, the area from the town of Yountville to the city of St. Helena is in the climatic region II, similar to Bordeaux. This area, with the town of Rutherford at the center, is California's Medoc. The fine Cabernets of Beaulieu, Inglenook, Heitz, Souverain, Freemark Abbey,

Spring Mountain, Robert Mondavi, Charles Krug, Chappellet, and Oakville Vineyards, are from grapes grown in this area. Some outstanding white wines are made both from Chardonnay and Sauvignon Blanc grapes grown in this section of the valley.

Climatically, the Napa Valley is an example, in miniature, of the great aero-dynamic system which operates in the bay area at large. The valley is one huge air corridor. The closed end of the valley, up against Mount St. Helena, being farther from the cooling bay air, is the warmest. The area in and around the town of Calistoga falls into region III. The rising warm air at this end of the valley draws air in from the bay, across Carneros, Napa, Rutherford and Saint Helena, exerting a cooling influence as it advances but also becoming warmer itself. Other cool air currents are funneled into the valley through canyons which cut through the Mayacamas Range. This creates a kind of infinite sliding scale of climatic gradations throughout the valley. The Napa Valley is certainly one of the most varied and incredible viticultural districts in the world.

There is perhaps no more lovely, more tranquil place than the quiet town of St. Helena on a warm, summer evening. The warmth radiating from the earth tempered by gentle zephyrs creates an extraordinary ambiance bringing delight and exhilaration.

As might be expected, there are some fine vineyards in the hills and mountains on either side of the valley. In the Mayacamas Range, the designations Napa and Sonoma fade into one another. Technically, most of the vineyards lie in Sonoma County, but the character of the wines seems to be more a part of Napa. Not without reason, Hugh Johnson lumps Napa and southern Sonoma together as a single viticultural region. Sonoma wines from the slopes which lead up to the Mayacamas Range seem to fall into the class of Napa wines. The gently rolling Sonoma Valley floor, though, is quite dissimilar from Napa and the wines have gained the reputation of being marvelous, honest, country-style wines. Although the future might prove me wrong, the potential seems not up to that of Napa.

There seems to be considerable potential, though, in the hills which rise above the west side of the valley, particularly in the area above the town of Glen Ellen. Before prohibition, this area was well developed and had gained an excellent reputation. Today there is a significant effort being made to revive this area at Grand Cru Vineyards.

There is another Sonoma County region which is fast gaining a reputation and identity of its own, the Alexander Valley/Dry Creek/Russian River region. It is quite distinct geographically from Sonoma/Napa, being a good 45 miles northwest of the city of Napa and a few miles north of the city of Santa Rosa. The Russian River has its source nearly 200 miles due north of Santa Rosa. It flows directly south from its source, unable to find a gap in the Coast Range until it reaches the Alexander Valley where it jogs around a hill, swings abruptly west, and meanders through low hills and redwood glens, until it finds the Pacific. It is this gap which provides a corridor for cool Pacific air. From the point where the river enters the north end of the Alexander Valley to the point where it snakes its way through redwood territory, there are two viticultural areas which can be distinguished. West of Highway 101 between Santa Rosa and Healdsburg (a distance of some 18 miles) there is an area of rich orchard land and vineyards set among gently undulating hills. This area is in region I. Just north of Healdsburg, there is a low range of hills which divides the lower Santa Rosa area from the Alexander Valley proper. This more northern area is in region II. Traveling north on 101, just beyond the Simi Winery and adjacent to the highway, one enters the valley, perhaps more like a broad, oval basin given over exclusively to the cultivation of the vine. The feeling of the place is reminiscent of the Napa Valley. Climatically the two areas are very similar. At the northern, tapering end of the valley, toward the town of Asti, the climate shades off into region III. The same climatic pattern as that of Napa is apparent: Carneros (region I) - Rutherford (region II) - Calistoga (region III); and, Santa Rosa (I) - Alexander Valley (II) - Asti (III). Alexander Valley wines have a very distinct and attractive *goût de terroir*. There is some gravelly/volcanic character to the soil; but, being a river basin, there is a good deal of alluvial silt from a river which has traveled through 200 miles of varied terrain. This is a viticultural area to watch very closely.

The vineyards among the hills which define the western rim of the valley have produced some very fine wines. Hidden in back of these hills is another narrow valley which runs parallel to the Alexander Valley, forming a third distinct viticultural area in this region—the Dry Creek area. Virtually every square inch of this lovely valley is devoted to the culture of vines. Dry Creek wines have a significant identity and character all their own. This is another area to watch closely.

Beginning several miles north of Asti, Mendocino County forms another distinct viticultural area, with its center at the City of Ukiah, 125 miles north of San Francisco. Although Ukiah is itself in region IV, the remarkably varied terrain of this area provides vineyard locations which shade well into region II, particularly to the west at the town of Philo. The wines from this extremely versatile region seem to benefit from the more northerly location.

Traveling in the opposite direction, south from San Francisco along the west side of San Francisco Bay, one can see a long, lateral slope which defines the western rim of the lengthy Santa Clara Valley. At South San Francisco the slope is rather low, making another one of those gaps which lets in ocean air. Driving out from the protection of San Bruno Mountain, the car is buffeted as it hits this "river" of air. If it is a summer afternoon one may see fog being swept along in the channel of air. Further south the slope rises almost imperceptibly. Tongues of fog lick the tops of the slope. Every few miles the air seems to warm by a degree or two as the slope becomes gradually higher. At a certain point there is a distinct resemblance to the Côte d'Or, but suburban homes dot the slope rather than vineyards. Hidden along the ridge at points which have escaped the upward sprawl of the bay area megalopolis are vineyards from which have come some of the finest Cabernets, Chardonnays, and Pinot Noirs made in California. Although the production is miniscule, the quality is so high that it demands special attention.

The eastern exposure of the vineyards is a key to the quality. The Santa Clara Valley is so wide and the vineyards so far above the valley floor that they are warmed by the sun very early in the morning. By early afternoon the vines are banked away from the intense rays of the overhead sun. Being so high up, there is excellent air circulation. The environment is remarkably similar to the Côte d'Or, although warmer. In this spectacular setting, grapes are grown for the fine Cabernet Sauvignons of Ridge and Gemello, and the Chardonnay and Pinot Noir of Mount Eden (formerly Martin Ray) and Dr. David Bruce among others.

Looking across the broad Santa Clara Valley from atop its eastern ridge one sees a low ridge of hills which defines the eastern slope of the valley. There are vineyards in the low slope which once belonged to Leland Stanford, founder of Stanford University.

To the south, beyond San Jose, there is an older viticultural section of the Santa Clara Valley which is currently undergoing a very positive revitalization.

Past the eastern slope of the valley one can just barely discern a broad oval basin of land, south of Mount Diablo, known as the Livermore Valley. In the era before prohibition, this valley with its gently rolling low hills and very porous, gravelly soil, attracted several homesick Frenchmen who found in the valley an environment which was remarkably similar to the Graves and Sauternes district of Bordeaux. The valley still prides itself on an old section of vineyard which was originally planted in the 19th century using cuttings from Chateau d'Yquem. The climate though, is warmer than Bordeaux (region III as opposed to region II) and the wines differ considerably from Bordeaux wines of the Graves and Sauternes districts. The superb white wines of Wente Brothers and Concannon Vineyards are quite unique and inimitable.

Livermore is one of the four vine growing valleys which form air corridors for the influx of cool ocean air through the Golden Gate. But at the northeast corner of the bay, near the city of Vallejo, the combined waters of the Sacramento and San Joaquin Rivers enter the bay through the Straits of Carquinas. Flowing through the central valley from the far north (Sacramento River) and from the far south (San Joaquin River) the two rivers finally meet at a point not far from the city of Lodi in the central valley. They meander in a broad delta region and then together they flow due west for some forty miles directly toward the bay. This forms a broad river valley which acts as a fifth important air corridor. (Drivers in the area will notice signs which warn: "Trucks and campers beware of high gusty winds next eight miles".) This flow of air has a tempering effect and provides good air circulation in the otherwise hot central valley section around the city of Lodi (region IV). Driving south on route 99, some ten miles between the town of Galt and the city of Lodi, one passes through a sea of vineyards. Vineyards in the Lodi district extend westward toward the peat bogs which surround the intersection of the Sacramento and San Joaquin Rivers, and eastward, virtually up to the beginning of the Sierra foothills. Not far beyond, some 1800 feet up in these foothills, is the Shenandoah Valley, with its old mining villages dating from gold rush days. This valley is also affected by the same bay air currents which affect Lodi. The climate is remarkably akin to that of the Italian Piedmont (high region III).

Lodi is the California counterpart of the Cognac district of Bordeaux, capable of producing some splendid wood aged brandies. Unfortunately, these brandies represent only a tiny percentage of brandy production, most of which is an awkwardly made product, doctored up with caramel. Lodi produces some fine Zinfandels and Ruby Cabernets (the U.C. hybrid of Cabernet Sauvignon and Carignane). Recently some intrepid growers have planted vineyards to Cabernet Sauvignon. It will be most interesting to follow the development of this experiment. Of the two regions, the Shenandoah Valley has produced by far the more interesting Zinfandels. Some of the vineyards here date back to the days of the gold rush, but there are also recent plantings to other grape varieties. Further developments in the Shenandoah Valley will certainly be worth watching very closely.

Approximately 100 miles directly south from San Francisco, there begins another important new viticultural district—Santa Cruz/Monterey/Salinas Valley. The broad sweep of Monterey Bay provides an opening for the ingression of cool air for the vineyards. There are important vineyards to the north of the bay in an area which ultimately connects into the southern tip of the Santa Clara Valley. Most of the remaining vineyards are in the Salinas Valley which stretches out from Monterey Bay in much the same way that the Santa Clara Valley extends southward from San Francisco Bay. There is the same gradation of regions I, II, and III.

There are several major differences, however. The soil makeup is based extensively on sand, providing excellent drainage and relatively little of the flavor elements which can be traced to the soil. If the wines are made well, they are generally very fruity and vinous. Another major difference is based on the structure of Monterey Bay. Sea air and fog does not enter through a narrow aperture as it does through the Golden Gate. The area surrounding Monterey Bay is more like a wide amphitheatre which sweeps up to the partially encircling Gavilan Mountains. Vineyards in the upper Salinas Valley are much more accessible to cool air and a wide blanket of fog which enters through Monterey Bay. Conditions are vaguely similar to those in the Sauternes and Barsac districts of Bordeaux and conditions along the Loire Valley in France; i.e., conditions which foster the development of a peculiar mold known as *botrytis cinerea*. Grapes do not spoil when they are attacked by this benign mold—rather, the mold creates a film or screen through which water evaporates while acid, extract and sugar remain. The wines are sweet, concentrated in flavor and have a peculiar rich and unctuous quality which sets them apart. The Monterey/Salinas Valley area has the potential of becoming California's answer to the Sauternes district of Bordeaux and the Coteaux du Layon of the Loire Valley, producing rich, immensely fruity dessert wines.

Unfortunately, much of the vineyard area is controlled by strictly commercial interests. The vines are heavily irrigated and overcropped and the wines are only marginally above the quality of bulk wines. Within a stone's throw of these vineyards, though, Wente, Chalone and from time to time Mirassou are making wines of exceptional quality. Dr. Richard Peterson, longtime associate of Andre Tchelistcheff, is also working to develop the higher potential of this area at Gerald Asher's Monterey Vineyards.

The Grower-Winery-Distributor

Relationship in California

Six

During the period from the end of prohibition to the early 1960's, the majority of California wineries were concentrating on the production of sound, marketable table wines. There was a kind of built-in inferiority complex, though, which assumed that California simply did not have the potential to compete with fine European wines on the same level of quality. Only Andre Tchelistcheff, Lee Stewart, and others previously mentioned had an unflinching faith that California was potentially one of the great wine districts of the world. For the majority, winemaking was strictly a commercial venture. Farmers grew the grapes and the wineries bought the grapes and turned them into wine—"after all, is that not what a winery is supposed to do?" The wineries were not particularly interested in the way the grapes were grown—"is not that, after all, the business of the farmer?" All the winemaker really cared about was that the grapes had sufficient sugar so that their juice could be turned into a marketable alcoholic beverage. Winemaking was considered just that—turning grapes of sufficient sweetness into wine.

There was no romance, no sophistication involved with the task. Wineries saw themselves as a link in a chain of responsibility with the rancher on the lower end providing grapes and the liquor wholesaler/distributor on the upper end marketing their product. The distributors, to whom the wineries were beholden, regarded wine as another alcoholic beverage, part of the product lineup which they had to offer to the restaurant and bar trade, the liquor shop trade and, in California, the grocery store trade. The distributors wanted a uniform product which would be as easy to sell as spirits.

There was a kind of naive democratization of wine, and the wineries were quite satisfied with the common denominator. Quality grapes and mediocre, over-cropped grapes were thrown together, willy-nilly. There was little effort to preserve or pursue individuality. Winemaking art, the effort to control and affect the highest quality at every step of the way, was rare. And yet, with prodding from the university and a very lively "intramural" competition, the wines managed to be generally sound and palatable.

When the premium wine boom hit in the early 1960's, most California wine producers were caught with their proverbial "pants" down. They were almost totally bewildered as the American palate suddenly became tremendously responsive to premium European wines. Imported wines captured a major percentage of the rapidly growing wine market in America.

Established wineries, at least, started their response by giving their attention to premium grape varieties. They realized that they had to work with Chardonnay, Johannisberg Riesling, Pinot Noir, Cabernet Sauvignon and other premium grapes in order to carve out a slice of the premium wine market. The general quality level improved but, unfortunately, premium grape varieties do not necessarily make premium wines. The wineries made the facile assumption that varietal wines were necessarily and by definition premium wines; and, at many wineries, this thinking persists to this day.

The supplies of premium grapes lagged far behind demand so that the wineries vied with each other to procure better varietal grapes. This, of course, drove the prices up very rapidly. It was a sellers' market. The grapes, although technically of a premium variety, were often over-cropped and of poor quality and condition.

The burden of tradition has weighed very heavily on the wine business in California. The hidebound thinking which separates winemaking from viticulture has persisted at many wineries even up to the present and is certainly one of the major reasons why premium wine is still somewhat the exception rather than the rule in California. Although lip service is paid to premium European wine, much of the parochialism of the 1950's persists.

The relation between the wineries and the growers has been a curious "cat-and-mouse" affair. Instances of close cooperation and mutual respect are not very common. The products of the growers are absorbed into a large pool of grapes, and whatever identity and special care might have been bred into the grapes is absorbed in the mass.[1] There is little chance for special pride to be taken in maintaining high quality standards.

Many wineries are insensitive to the nuances of soil and micro-climate which can differentiate a complex of vineyards and give character and individuality to the wines. Beyond the simple designation of the five regions, there has been very little further research into the complex set of differences in soil makeup and micro-climate variation in California.

Many wineries are so backward in their understanding of viticultural matters that they are unable to distinguish one grape variety from another on sight. There have been known instances of wineries mistakenly accepting inferior grape varieties for premium varieties. This has only bred further lack of respect on the part of the growers.

There is one major controlling factor in this situation and that is the manner which the price is set for wine grapes in California. Some growers are under long term special contract with certain wineries, but the majority are under short term contract (one to three years). A few intrepid growers dispense altogether with contracts and sell their grapes to the highest bidder at harvest. Most grower-winery contracts are tied to what is called the "going rate", established each year for each different grape variety. The going rate is a standard dollar amount per ton of grapes, harvested and delivered to the winery. Production levels for each grape variety at each winery are more or less pre-established, based on sales trends, existing inventory, available equipment and cooperage. Short term demand can be determined fairly easily. Supply is determined by the actual tonnage at the completion of the harvest. Several weeks after the harvest, the going rate is

---

[1] I have heard this system jokingly referred to as "the game of grape roulette".

set, based on the year's supply and demand for each variety. Most contracts between individual wineries and individual growers stipulate that the price paid will be set according to the going rate. Recently, some contracts have also stipulated that a bonus be paid for grapes with a brix reading of over 22° (for red wine grapes) and a penalty against the established price for grapes which fall below 22° brix. Generally there is no further stipulation as to the quality of the grapes.

The result is obvious. With a given recommended price per ton of grapes, there is a temptation on the part of the growers to stretch tonnage to the maximum by over-cropping and by last minute irrigation.

Growers will tend to leave the grapes on the vine as long as possible to get the high sugar bonus. The growers' only restraining factor is the fear of rain which might cause a dramatic reduction in the sugar level of their grapes or else cause bunch rot and spoilage. Low acid and high alcohol wines are more often the result, lacking in balance and the zesty acidity appropriate to table wine. Many connoisseurs complain of this general characteristic in California wine, assuming that it must be the result of the hot California sunshine; while actually it is the wineries' insistence on the highest possible sugar in the grapes, which is one of the major contributing factors. What should be a rational decision of the winemaker based on aesthetics, is often a decision made for him by "the system".

I have heard some winemakers complain that sugar *has* to be well over 22° or else the pigmentation of the wine will be poor. What such a winemaker actually fears is that the additional time the wine would have to ferment on the skins to get the desired pigment would result in too much tannin. The wine would take too long to age and the consumers who normally buy from him would turn to less tannic wines. Of course, if the grapes were fine in all other respects, the wine might turn out to be far better, far more balanced when the tannin recedes.

More often than not, the growers, not understanding the importance of sugar/acid balance in winemaking, pick and deliver at their own discretion rather than working closely with the winemaker. This often throws any careful planning out of phase and the vintage is hectic and disorganized. Faced with the responsibility of making anywhere from 15 to 25 different wines in the "product line", it is no wonder the winemaker finds the vintage difficult to organize properly! Among the exceptions is Brother Timothy's carefully planned, beautifully organized winemaking operation at Christian Brothers; truly a model for California. Christian Brothers has traditionally demanded and received more stringent specifications on the grapes it buys and has gained special respect from the growers.

By 1973, supplies of premium grape varieties were beginning to catch up with demand and in 1975 California experienced a significant surplus of premium grapes. Wineries became much less intimidated and far more fussy about the grapes they bought. In the 1974 vintage, some wineries paid special bonuses for quality factors other than sugar readings for the first time. This is a very late beginning, but a beginning nonetheless.

Because of the general dichotomy of grape growing and winemaking, the growers and the wineries were never willing or able to sit down together to chart general directions and long term objectives, and attempt to bring some ordered growth into the hectic California wine scene. The general viewpoint has traditionally been very short sighted. As the prices for certain varieties rose dramatically, there was a big rush to "get in on the bonanza" and plant vineyards to those varieties. Only cursory attention was given to the suitability of the soil and micro-climate for the grape variety. Few growers realized that with everyone else trying to get in on the action, short supply might eventually turn into oversupply and depressed prices. This pattern has repeated itself so often in California that one would think that the lesson would have been learned.

In spite of all these problems, California is producing a great deal of fair to good, highly marketable wine with pretentions to premium quality.

Most of the established wineries have managed to prosper. They invoke the immortal words of George F. Babbit, "Nothing succeeds quite like success!" Unfortunately, relatively few seem to understand that, not just *good* wine, but superb to great wine could be made in several of California's viticultural areas as a matter of course, and that the world might be waiting at its doorstep with each succeeding vintage. *But given the present set of circumstances and the present system of doing things at many of the wineries, there is simply no way that such an objective could be made a reality.*

Many established wineries are confronted with serious competition from several sources. For one thing, the production of quality bulk wines in the central valley has developed and improved to the extent that bulk wines are often better value (and in some instances are actually better wines at half the price) than many of the so-called "premium" wines which are part of a cumbersome product line.

The university has devoted a great deal of attention to the technology of bulk wine production. This has been a reasonable, even laudable, priority. The enjoyment and appreciation of truly premium wines is perhaps best given a solid foundation in the enjoyment and appreciation of good everyday beverage wine. And furthermore, most of the jobs for graduates of the university have been in the bulk wine industry. Perhaps the time has come, though, for the university to give premium winemaking its fair share of attention. It is far behind the French and German universities in this respect.

There will always be plenty of room for varietal wines of reasonable quality and character at appropriately lower prices. Sebastiani Winery makes an outstanding contribution followed, perhaps, by Louis Martini, Pedroncelli, Wente and Italian Swiss Colony in the north coast and Gallo and Giumarra in the central valley. These few wineries bend backwards to provide value for money in most of their products while others build a reputation on one or two fine wines and then try to pin a whole string of mediocre wines at inflated prices onto that reputation.

In spite of the system, with each succeeding vintage there seems to be more and more premium quality wines being made in California. Unfortunately, these wines have to be hunted down and chosen with great care, usually with the help of an astute wine merchant and/or one of the better monthly wine newsletters. There are several winemakers who are finding their way around the problems and obstacles which I have outlined, particularly the grower-winery antithesis; and, even more importantly, *we are beginning to see an increasing number of wines which are carefully made and quality controlled by the winemaker from the ground up.* What, then, are the conditions under which these truly premium wines are being made in California?

Some patterns were set early in the establishment of small estates, where vineyards most suitable to the growing of premium grapes were carefully chosen and a small estate built up, often from scratch; equipment was carefully designed to produce the finest quality possible in wines which would reflect the individuality and taste of the owner. Such was Hanzell Vineyards, the creation of J. D. Zellerbach in association with Brad Webb. In some instances, the owner was also the grower and the winemaker. Such were the Mayacamas Estate, a creation of John and Mary Taylor who not only tended the vines but made the wines as well; and Fred and Eleanor McCrea's single handed creation of the Stony Hill estate. More recently Richard Graff, with the help of a few enthusiastic investors, has built Chalone Vineyards (Monterey County) into one of the finest small "chateau" wineries in California. Donn Chappellet and Dr. David Bruce are other somewhat heroic winemakers who have built small "chateau" wineries, making wines of high quality with an individual, inimitable stamp. Michael and Arlene Bernstein have been developing their Mount Veeder Winery, high in the Mayacamas Range, for the past several years.

For many years now, Mike Robbins has been building up his own estate—Spring Mountain Vineyards. But while the new vines are coming up to full production, he has made special arrangements with other growers and wineries to produce wines for him, following his specifications. Mike has cared for and finished these wines, among them some of the finest Chardonnays made in the Napa Valley. Alfred Baxter at Veedercrest Vineyards is doing much the same thing.

Following the lead of Mike Robbins, the Joseph Phelps Vineyard (Napa), soon to come into production, launched the name of the winery with one of the finest Johannisberg Rieslings yet to be made in California, using grapes purchased from the Stanton Ranch in the Carneros district. Dave Stare's Dry Creek Vinyards will soon come into production, but in the meantime, Dave has won the respect of his neighboring growers and he has made some fine wines from their grapes. (I mention these estates as examples—other grower/winemakers are following this pattern as well.)

An alternative to this somewhat heroic approach was a more complex arrangement whereby a small association of growers, committed to growing the finest quality premium grapes in carefully selected, carefully tended vineyards, developed a special working relationship with a winemaker and winery owner equally committed to premium quality wine. Such an arrangement was the relationship of Zinfandel Associates vineyards with the Joe Heitz winery. Here, a mutual commitment to produce extraordinary Cabernet Sauvignon and Chardonnay has obviated all of the problems which have beset most grower-winery relationships. Everyone concerned, Dr. and Mrs. Robert Adamson, Dr. and Mrs. Bernard Rhodes, Joe Heitz and others went far beyond the parochialism of the California scene, developing their enterprises out of a deep understanding and appreciation of the culture of wine. In many ways, they set the tone, the pace, and the quality level for premium wine production in California. Unfortunately, but necessarily, the production is small. Heitz and his associates proved that the entire production could be sold at the winery and in a few selected shops which specialized in fine wine, without the help of a distributor who might put special demands on the way the wine was made.

Several premium wine enthusiasts became interested in developing vineyards along the pattern set by Zinfandel Associates while other enthusiasts became part- or full-time winemakers, devoted to making a few wines of premium qualtiy. Small wineries such as Z-D of Sonoma, working with dedicated ranchers in the Carneros district of Napa, have followed this pattern. Chateau Montelena (Napa) has been able to develop a particularly successful rapport with several quality conscious ranchers in the Napa and Alexander Valleys.

In the early 1960's, two fine organizations evolved which committed themselves to building premium wine "estates" on a fairly large scale; namely, Freemark Abbey and Sterling Vineyards. Freemark Abbey was founded by a group of dedicated enthusiasts who had consonant tastes in wine and who pooled their resources, planting out their own extensive acerage to premium grapes and designing special winery facilities which would accommodate the products of their vineyards. Both Sterling and Freemark Abbey have combined quality control all along the line with long range, planned objectives. We are only beginning to see the fruits of their careful planning, investment and hard work.

Perhaps most important of all, these two wineries have proved that fine, premium quality wine can be made in significantly larger quantities, that the *small* estate is not a necessary condition for the production of truly premium wine. In fact, a few of these small estates have made some decidedly inferior wines. Often they take the wines so personally that they seem intent on marketing their less successful wines at high prices rather then selling them off for blending into bulk wines where they belong.

Some of the more established wineries built a niche for premium wine within their existing shell of commercial operation, concentrating on one, two or three premium varietals and producing extraordinary products cheek and jowl with their commercial "line". Such are the Cabernets and Chardonnays of Charles Krug, the Cabernets of Inglenook and the Cabernet, Pinot Noir, and Chardonnay of Beaulieu. The commercial products helped to underwrite the more costly production of their chosen premium wine and served as a hedge in the event of its failure. The commercial end of the "line" served to facilitate distribution. They had thrown their lot in with the liquor distributor and had to play his game up to a point. Peter Mondavi at Krug had faithfully maintained a strong commitment to produce one of the finest California Cabernets for more than two decades. However, recent vintages do not seem to be up to these earlier standards. I need only mention the wine masterpieces of Andre Tchelistcheff at Beaulieu. Unfortunately, Inglenook has attempted to tie its entire "line" to its only wine of consistently premium quality (Cabernet Sauvignon), passing off many utterly banal wines as premium ones. The tragedy is that the precious acreage which is devoted to second rate varietals, in the name of the "complete product line", could have been replanted to the one varietal grape from which they could make a fine wine.

Of course, these wineries will probably always find enough consumers who do not shop carefully and become sold on the brand name. Knowledgeable consumers simply cannot rely on faith in the brand to buy fine wine. They can, however, take advantage of the situation. While many of the wines in the line represent poor value, the wines upon which the house bases its reputation often represent exceptional value. The costs of these superior wines have been spread over the entire line.

Being a long term investment, both large and small wineries need adequate capitalization to become viable. A few independents, severely bitten by wine fever, launched small premium wine operations with less than adequate funding. Some were dedicated individualists; others, hoping that corporate funding would take them under its umbrella, looked to make a major splash in the market. Dick Lynn, one of the dedicated individualists, attracted one of the more promising of the younger winemakers, John Henderson, and launched Lyncrest Vineyards in a blaze of glory. The lack of adequate funding, the recession, and fierce competition drove the operation to bankruptcy.

Other independents such as Joseph Phelps and Eli Calloway had, not only ample personal wealth, but keen palates and extraordinary enthusiasm. Both have launched small wineries which show great promise.

Another, perhaps unsuspected, development has turned out to be highly significant. A few growers who had an abiding love of fine wine and had developed their ranches very conscientiously, became heart-broken as year after year their fine grapes were absorbed into the mass, losing all identity, or else ruined by inept winemaking or poor cooperage. Some of those who had enough foresight to develop vineyards of premium grape varieties were holding back small lots of their fruit to try their hand at winemaking, producing enough for their own personal consumption. Many were discovering that their own homemade product was remarkably superior to the commercial wines into which their grapes were absorbed. Out of experiences such as these has evolved a new kind of estate winery which produces very individual, artfully made wines, many of extraordinary quality. Most of these independents have disproved the proposition that a costly melange of sophisticated equipment—centrifuges, temperature controlled fermentation vats, special filters, etc.—is absolutely necessary in order to make premium wine.

These small estates have eschewed the customary product line and concentrated on a few premium varietals. Because they made the wines very carefully from the ground up, they had enough confidence in themselves not to need the crutch of a product line. These same grower/winemakers, understanding the frustration of other conscientious growers, have been able to attract the products of the better ranches. At least the ranchers could deal with someone who understood their problems and aspirations. They could be assured that special, individual qualities would not be blended into a common denominator.

Ridge Vineyards is perhaps the prototype of this kind of winery. Among others are the small Caymus Winery of Charles Wagner and Warren Winiarski's Stag's Leap Wine Cellars (both in the Napa Valley); Joseph Swan Vineyards in Forestville (Sonoma County) and Frank Bartholemew's new Hacienda Vineyards, just outside the town of Sonoma. Wagner has shown winemakers who have been struggling for years with Pinot Noir just how to manage this scrawny, recalcitrant varietal, not by accident, but by a thorough understanding of the grape, at every step of the way, from the planting out of the vines to the finished product.

Ridge Vineyards has probably blazed more trails in the area of premium wine than any other winery in California. Instead of sitting on their hands at the small estate winery high above Cupertino, Paul Draper and his colleagues are out in the California vineyards, seeking out growers who take special care and pride in their products, whose grapes have special, individual qualities which warrant special and separate attention such as Fritz Maytag's York Creek Vineyards on Spring Mountain (Napa) and the Eisele ranch near Calistoga which is devoted to Cabernet and Chardonnay.

As more and more growers demand some kind of recognition for the special qualities which they have nurtured in their grapes, and as wineries begin to see the validity of their demands, marketing managers and distributors connected with the larger wineries make a big fuss. They argue that all the complications of labeling, of keeping several lots of the same grape variety separate, would create an absurd distribution tangle and a paperwork nightmare. The public wants product uniformity, they insist.

Certainly the public wants product uniformity when it comes to soap or motor oil or even *vin ordinaire*—but premium wines? Lovers of fine wine taste for *differences*, not for boring sameness! Truly premium wine —carefully and individually crafted wine of exceptional quality—is one of the few remaining sources of enjoyment in our industrialized society which can escape the heavy hand of "product standardization", be widely shared and enjoyed, and yet remain within the means of so many people.

On the other hand, no matter how high an art form winemaking can become, it is still a business. The wines must be distributed and sold through some set of channels if they are to exist as anything beyond homemade products. Channels of distribution have a profound effect on the wines.

I have already discussed the genesis of the product line philosophy *vis à vis* wine distribution: how California wine has been "piggy-backed" into the wine and spirits stores and restaurants by the liquor distributors. But as the American wine drinking palate has become more sophisticated we have seen many new shops and merchants who specialize in premium quality wine, buying wines according to intrinsic quality and not according to brand. The growth of the small "chateau" type winery which produces individual wines has developed hand in hand with these new avenues of distribution. The two have been more or less interdependent. Merchants seek out wines with special qualities rather than rubber stamp wines, as a service to their discriminating clientele. For the most part, it is the small winery which accommodates them.

Often these merchants will publish a newsletter, to keep their customers informed. Several merchants are providing a wine tasting bar where premium wines can be bought and sampled by the glass. A few of these specialized wine shops, though, have been complete humbug, easily recognized by a few tell-tale signs: a clerk who is unable to discuss wine intelligently will be decked out with a silver-plated chain and tastevin hanging around his neck; every effort has been made to generate snob appeal, and most of the prices will be from 5% to 25% higher than any self-respecting wine merchant would ask.

Wineries that tie their distribution in with the liquor distributors have to accommodate their products to the needs of the distributor, his retailers and the retailers' customers. In this channel, the consumer does not have the benefit of the experience and good taste of a knowledgeable merchant. Advertised brands, shelf-space saturation, point-of-sale gimmicks, these must suffice. Naturally, an array of Zinfandels with different vineyard designations but from the same winery would be confusing and perhaps embarrassing for the distributor, the retailer and the consumer. In such a situation, the winemaker feels constrained to provide wines which will offend no one.

It would be an ultimate piece of snobbery to assume that wines of any character can only be found at a specialized wine merchant. There is most assuredly a place for branded wines of somewhat less than the highest premium quality which one buys on a day to day basis at the nearby grocery or liquor store. Sebastiani, Louis Martini, Wente, Christian Brothers, Italian Swiss Colony and Gallo have proved that wine of good character and reasonable value for money can be provided through this channel. Almaden and Paul Masson have provided excellent jug wines through their vast national distribution network. Gallo, especially, has become a master in the art of mass-marketing and distributing wine—but they have not let these conditions compromise reasonable character and excellent value. Gallo wines have provided a solid base for countless people to acquire a taste for wine and incorporate it into their regular diet. Gallo has its own distribution network and does an imaginative, aggressive job of marketing while the liquor distributors and jobbers seem to be sitting on their hands. No wonder Gallo has captured 40% of the market for California wine!

Much of the fate of California wines, especially the premium wines, is tied to the ways in which California wine producers will surmount the very special and incredible problems involved in distributing their wines *nationally*. With the repeal of prohibition, Congress assigned to each state the responsibility to create its own set of laws regulating the production, distribution and sale of alcoholic beverages. To this day, there is an incredible tangle of laws *within each state*. Any two sets of laws bear only the vaguest resemblance to each other. Because no federal guidelines were set down, the fifty sets of laws governing the states are completely heterogeneous. There exists a massive tangle of fees, protective tariffs, regulations and paperwork requirements which make it virtually impossible for the smaller, quality conscious wineries to export to other states.

For a California winery to undertake even limited national distribution it must have a considerable *quantity* of wine in order to make large shipments and in order to spread all the costs over a large enough quantity of wine so that the additional costs per case or bottle do not run the price up beyond competitive levels. Production would have to be such that the quantity of the various wine types could be increased or decreased with the fluctuations of demand. Rather than committing products to a 100% varietal composition, extensive blending is usually necessary to adjust supplies of various varietal wines as they become more or less popular. California law requires that only 51% of the named variety need be used to make the wine. Naturally, the producers of nationally distributed wines take full advantage. Blending for aesthetic reasons is one thing, blending in neutral wines which contribute little and sap the individuality from the other 51% is quite another. Such wines will seldom be very interesting or satisfying.

The 51% varietal composition law is urgently in need of modification. It is my own belief that if a wine is given a varietal designation and it is not 100% of the variety, one should be entitled to know the makeup of the blend. If a Chardonnay, for example, is blended out with another premium varietal such as Pinot Blanc, that is all well and good. It may make a great deal of aesthetic good sense and nobody would object. However, if it is blended with a worthless, purely neutral wine made from Thompson Seedless grapes, then the consumer should know this and not be misled into paying a premium price for such an adulterated wine.

Producers of nationally distributed wines have also felt obliged to maintain programs of rigid product standardization. It is extremely difficult to do this and still retain a reasonable degree of character in the wine. Gallo and perhaps Christian Brothers have managed to straddle the fence. For most others, character and individuality are sacrificed to product standardization except, perhaps, for one or two of the wines in the product line.

Consumers outside the state of California should realize that most astute California shoppers can often find wines comparable to the nationally distributed brands at half the price. I buy several very nice jug white and jug red wines for everyday consumption at less than $3.00 per gallon. True, it took some shopping to find the jugs I like at the price I like to pay but such bargains are not uncommon in California. Winelovers across the country should realize that there are major additional costs involved in national distribution; *but* they should also realize that they are paying a substantial additional premium because of a bureaucratic tangle of unjust state laws governing the sale and distribution of table wine. Even more tragic is the way in which these laws are choking off the distribution of the finest premium wines. Very few of these wines ever leave the state of California.

There are some channels of national distribution for premium California wine which have been able to surmount these problems. There are some wine merchants in the larger cities (e.g., Calvert in Washington D.C. and Martin's Wine Cellar in New Orleans) who do their own selective importing of California premium wines. Consumers who patronize wine merchants who *are* large enough to do their own importing of California premium wines should demand that they do so. There is enough premium wine made in California today to warrant their doing this selective importing. For smaller merchants who are unable to do this, it is obvious that what is needed is some sort of counterpart to the French "négociant" or the "special selections" system such as that of Frederick Wildman. We have the beginnings of such a system of selection and national distribution of California premium wines in the Seattle (Washington) based organization Bon-Vin, Inc. California is capable of producing all the premium wine necessary to satisfy the needs of a discriminating national market, but only as those avenues of distribution which are *selective* open up, will California be producing premium wine as a matter of course and wine lovers throughout the United States will be enjoying them. This will take time.

With regard to the laws which govern the production and distribution of wines, it is time, perhaps, for an enlightened consumerism which would demand some reasonable changes. Unfortunately, much of the consumerism to date has concerned itself with such relatively unimportant objectives as demand for labeling which lists any additives to wines.

Consumers in California and some other states are saddled with fair trade laws which maintain minimum prices at which wines can be sold. These laws are generally maintained under the influence of a strong industry lobby. Legislators sanctimoniously justify the laws, arguing that the high prices protect consumers from becoming alcoholics, refusing to acknowledge that wine is a major civilizing influence. The sooner that consumers demand that such laws be thrown out, the better.

Perhaps it would be too quixotic an endeavor for consumers to demand that some order be brought into the welter of laws, regulations and protective tariffs which impede the distribution of premium quality table wine. The very significant *aesthetic* value of table wine certainly provides the motive for such a cause, however impractical or impossible it may seem.

There is perhaps a great deal which wine lovers and consumers can do within each state, especially in demanding adjustment to laws which fail to recognize that table wine is a significantly different kind of alcoholic beverage. Because table wine is also a *food*, an *artistic* entity, and a *major civilizing influence*, it would not be unreasonable for consumers to demand that table wine be given special status.

Dry table wine does not really come under the American concept of "the drink" (as in "let's have a drink" or "let's go out drinking tonight"). There is a natural limiting function built into table wine. Table wine makes sense mainly as an accompaniment to food. Because of its acidic character, one is not so inclined to drink table wine on its own in excessive amounts. And because table wine is consumed with food, the impact of alcohol is greatly mollified. Because it *does* have an alcoholic content, table wine is subject to abuse but not nearly to the extent that other alcoholic beverages are subject to abuse.

It would not be unreasonable for consumers and producers alike to demand that table wine be given special status. Consumers will be rewarded by better quality wines at far more reasonable prices, producers would benefit from the increased volume of business and governments would benefit from reasonable taxes, additional jobs and the health and well-being of its citizens.

Perhaps the words of Thomas Jefferson will be sufficient to answer all objections:

> No nation is drunken where wine is cheap, and none sober where the dearness of wine substitutes ardent spirits as the common beverage.
>
> I think it is a great error to consider a heavy tax on wines, as a tax on luxury. On the contrary, it is a tax on the health of our citizens. Surely it is not from the necessities of our treasury that we thus undertake to debar the mass of our citizens from the use of not only an innocent gratification, but a healthy substitute instead of a bewitching poison. This aggression on the public taste and comfort has been ever deemed among the most arbitrary and oppressive abuses of the English government. It is one which, I hope, we shall never copy.
>
> The introduction of a very cheap wine into my neighborhood, within two years past, has quadrupled in that time the

number of those who keep wines and will ere long increase them tenfold. This would be a great gain to the treasury, and to the sobriety of our country.

We have not had an enlightened consumerism with regard to table wine in this country. Much of the "consumerism" has come from a vociferous group of faddists who have demanded labels which would list trace additives to the wines. There *are* certain legitimate additives, traditionally accepted and necessary in the winemaking process. *Safe levels of these additives are strictly limited and controlled by existing laws.* The demand that these trace additives be listed on the label is as silly as demanding that butchers label all meat packages with a chemical analysis of the dye used for the U.S.D.A. stamp. Wine is not the kind of standardized product which lends itself to such labeling. For any of these additives to have an adverse effect on health, it would be necessary for a person to imbibe such vast quantities of wine that he would be stricken with cirrhosis of several livers before the effect would be felt.

The Federal Bureau of Alcohol, Tobacco and Firearms has wisely and responsibly rejected this demand. Let us hope that the matter will rest there. Such a requirement would have no effect on quality and would provide no actual benefit to consumers. It might even have a major adverse effect. It would force consumer prices up and, in addition, neither the smaller wineries nor foreign producers would be willing or able to comply with such a ridiculous requirement. Winelovers might wake up one day to find that the Burgundy and Bordeaux bins at their wine shop were empty.

Enlightened consumers should encourage the development of *appellation contrôllée* laws with regard to California and other American wines. They should realize, though, that European laws do far more than merely guarantee that a wine came from a certain district. It also guarantees that the wine was made from grapes grown on vines which have been pruned to production levels appropriate to premium wine. It guarantees that only premium grape varieties are used and that the quality is acceptable to a board of review which includes representatives from the industry, the government and the university. Any *appelation contrôllée* laws which would simply guarantee district of origin would be of very limited, perhaps negligible, value and would not warrant the additional cost to consumers.

Table wine is under the jurisdiction of the Federal Bureau of Alcohol, Tobacco and Firearms (strange bedfellows indeed!) which itself is a branch of the Treasury Department. The problem lies in the fact that there is no existing government organ which is able to claim adequate and intelligent jurisdiction over all of the basic aspects of wine and their legal ramifications: wine as *food*, wine as *alcohol*, and wine as an *object of art*. It seems to me that wine should be granted special legal status with its own governmental organ of jurisdiction, as it is in many European wine-producing countries.

Table wine, more than any other alcoholic or non-alcoholic beverage, gives us a unique human value—it is a major contributor to the joy, the conviviality and the shared delight of the dinner table. Consumers should demand the right to share freely in this unique human value, without impedance from unreasonable laws.

Part Two

California Premium Wine:

The Major Varietals

Introduction

As Harry Waugh has pointed out, there are basically two ways to write about wines—either one gives over-all descriptions of wine "types" and makes vague generalities about them or else one gets down to cases and discusses individual wines. Most connoisseurs seem to agree that it is far more interesting and instructive to read about specific wines. After all, wine flows across flesh and blood palates and not across "general" palates. Wine resists our attempts to generalize too much about it.

Furthermore, no wine is a static, finished object. Wine develops and changes character to a remarkable degree over a period of time. Wine is characteristically and inevitably a living thing. But this presents a major problem for the writer who describes specific wines in a full length book. By the time the tasting notes get into print, the wines have gone on to develop—either for better or for worse. And, what is often the case; by the time the book is in the hands of readers, most of the best wines have been snapped up by alert and informed consumers. This is particularly true of California wines, since there is not nearly enough wine of exceptional quality to go around.

Certainly, we need up-to-date and accurate descriptions and educated guesses on the aging potential of young wines as guides to our purchases and our investments in premium quality wines. There are many professional wine people who make it their business to provide just that kind of guidance: reputable wine merchants, writers of private wine letters, writers of news columns on wine, and publishers of wine magazines. The information and advice which they provide can be invaluable. These people put their professional reputation on the line for the accuracy of their descriptions and predictions and the usefulness of their advice. The truth of their statements and the compatability of their tastes with one's own will be borne out sooner or later.

As far as *this* book is concerned, it has not been my intention to write a buyer's guide. My objective in the next six chapters is mainly to describe various wines which are representative of the finer wines of their type, to discuss specific problems related to the making of these types of wine, and to work toward a definition of the major varietal wines of California. The purpose of describing specific wines need not be limited to guiding consumers in their purchases. We also need tasting notes which describe in depth those wines which have come to maturity and have been particularly fine and successful examples of their type—wines which have set the pace and have given us some idea of the upper range of possibilities. I have not given much attention to the common denominator of the wines. It is my belief that those wines which are the most desirable for one reason or another are the ones which establish in our minds a definition of a certain type of wine. By describing these finer wines in some depth, I have sought to frame, not a "scientific", but a practical, working definition of the major varietals which will give the reader some idea of what to look for in the premium varietal wines.

In selecting specific wines for discussion, I have not tried to choose wines which I thought were "the best" on an absolute scale. I am not trying to establish any kind of hierarchy or "*cru classé*". Wines can be remarkable and desirable in many ways—not only for their intrinsic excellence but for their versatility or their exceptional value for money or for their uncompromising expression of a winemaker's individual taste and point of view. Often the "best" wines, on an absolute scale, are the wines which are so rare and/or expensive that most of us never get to taste them. I have also avoided discussing wines which, in spite of their excellence, are produced in such small quantities that it is almost impossible to find them. I have purposely neglected other exceptional wines which have already received a great deal of attention—the Cabernets of Joe Heitz, for example, have been written up so well by Harry Waugh, Gerald Asher and many others, that I simply had nothing significant to add to their comments.

All of the wines which I discuss were acquired through normal channels—no special tastings were arranged for me. Most of the wines were tasted at various points in their state of development in order that the final assessment might be made when the wines were showing their full potential.

Most of the wines were consumed at table with appropriate foods. I have followed the French theory which holds that one adds significantly to the description of a wine if one gives a food context in which the wine has shown exceptionally well. This is based on the principle that wines at one level of sophistication, complexity and general quality show best with foods which have similar and complementary levels of sophistication, complexity and quality. Given the appropriate level of food, then, one can get a fair idea of the level of quality and sophistication of the wine.

I have also not hesitated to make comparisons between California and European wines of the same type. Several professional writers have cautioned strongly against making such comparisons but I suspect that they do this more for reasons of diplomacy than for any other reason. It is important to assess California wines on their own terms and not judge them positively only to the extent that they have marked similarities to European wines. As Kathleen Bourke put it, one has to "re-calibrate the taste buds" when making such comparisons.

The consumer inevitably makes such comparisons if only to make intelligent buying decisions. If he owns both California and European wines of the same type he might well enjoy serving the two together as a study in contrast. As long as he has some notion of the differing conditions under which the two are produced, he can detach his palate sufficiently to make unbiased comparisons. I have made it a point, in discussing the varietals, to give some idea of these differing conditions. Often, certain advantages and handicaps which affect the European wines balance out a different set of advantages and disadvantages in California. There will be differences in style and approach but the over-all desirability of one over the other might not be very great. Imaginative people will find uses for both at their table.

I have also made comparisons for the benefit of those connoisseurs who are more familiar with European wines than with California wines. This will provide an outside frame of reference so that such a reader can better understand my descriptions of California wines.

I should add one final word of warning. In praising a wine of a specific vintage, the reader should not conclude that the wine will be as fine in subsequent vintages. The 1968 Beaulieu Pinot Noir, for example, is perhaps one of the finest Pinot Noirs ever made in California. This has not prevented at least one more recent Beaulieu Pinot Noir from being among the poorest.

There are constant and significant changes going on in the California wine scene—changes of ownership, changes of winemaker, loss of contracts with growers, the acquisition of new equipment, etc. And, of course, each different vintage year brings significant variations in weather conditions which affect the wines (although perhaps less so in California than in Europe). All of these changes can have a considerable impact on quality and it is important for the interested consumer to keep up with the changes through wine columns in newspapers, wine letters, magazines and conversation with one's merchant.

A change of ownership can often provide badly needed capital and equipment and breathe new life into an older winery. Look, for example, at the strides which Beringer wines have taken since the Nestlé acquisition and Myron Nightingale was appointed winemaker. On the other hand, a change of ownership can also mean that an investor simply wants to milk the good name and reputation of the former owner for a short term profit and then run the business into the ground. Few would deny that this, too, is happening at certain wineries in California.

Now that Phil Baxter (formerly winemaker at Charles Krug) has taken over from Lee Stewart at Souverain Cellars (Napa), we can expect the wines to have a somewhat different style from the wines which Stewart made. Compare, for example, Stewart's 1970 Souverain Cellars Zinfandel with Baxter's 1971 Souverain Cellars Zinfandel. Both are exceptionally fine wines but there are significant differences in style. One might also compare the older Concannon (Livermore) wines with those of the 1974 vintage. The Concannons have recently made a major investment in new equipment and this has affected a considerable improvement in the quality of their wines.

California Cabernet Sauvignon

Seven

Cabernet Sauvignon is the grape variety which is used extensively to make the fine red wines of Bordeaux. Hard and disagreeably sharp in its younger years, a wine made primarily from Cabernet Sauvignon can develop an extraordinary bouquet and flavor. One must have patience and discipline to let the wine come up to its potential.

Cabernet Sauvignon vineyards were not planted in California on any significant scale until the 1880's. Gustave Niebaum at Inglenook (Rutherford, Napa Valley) was the undisputed leader. His Extra Fine Claret, made from Cabernet Sauvignon, gained and held its reputation as the finest red wine made in California.

From Prohibition up until, say, 1960, there were some fine California wines made from Cabernet Sauvignon, but only a few far-sighted individuals had the patience and understanding to put these wines away in their cellars to age them properly. Most Californians had no idea of the potential of the wines, with the result that the fine Cabernet Sauvignons of Beaulieu (Napa), for example, were unable to fetch more than $2.00 per bottle. Tax laws were a major stumbling block. Up until very recently, the state of California levied a yearly inventory tax on all wines in bottle held at the winery. This tax made it virtually impossible for the winemaker to hold on to his Cabernets while they developed bottle age.

By the early 1960's, American wine lovers were discovering the great red Bordeaux and were learning to cellar these fine wines. Eventually, they brought the same discipline to bear on California Cabernet Sauvignon. It is only recently that many wine lovers are getting an accurate, general picture of the range of possibilities of California Cabernet. Fortunately, a few cognoscenti who had been collecting California Cabernets dating back to the 1930's have shared their treasures with that extraordinary British wine critic, Harry Waugh. We have the limited satisfaction of reading his tasting notes on these rare wines, written while the excitement and shock of discovery was still vivid.

At this point, it is virtually safe to say that Cabernet makes the finest red wine in California, *provided that it is left to mature properly.* All too often, one hears of the lamentable experience of novice wine drinkers who, having heard that Cabernet Sauvignon is the best California red, and having paid the premium price, poured it for a special occasion, only to be greatly disappointed in the harsh and unattractive character of the wine. Fortunately, there is now some well aged Cabernet Sauvignon available at a few selected wine shops, and although the price is generally high, it is worth the investment to discover what all the fuss is about. The experience should demonstrate the rewards of laying down California Cabernet Sauvignon.

Because most Cabernets had been drunk young, all sharing the sameness of young wine, it was generally assumed that different vintages did not produce markedly different wine. Now that there has been enough Cabernet left to mature properly, we are beginning to see how these wines can differ considerably, both within each vintage and from vintage to vintage.

As Bordeaux is in the center of region II, it has not been surprising that the finest California Cabernets also come from region II. In the Napa/Sonoma area there is a Cabernet "belt" which is roughly fifteen miles on either side of a line drawn through the town of Sonoma and the village of Rutherford in the Napa Valley. It includes the mountain vineyards of Louis Martini, Mayacamas and Chappellet as well as the Napa Valley vineyards which cluster about the town of Rutherford. Recently some fine Cabernets have been made from warmer vineyards close to Calistoga. This does not necessarily argue for the superiority of the grapes, but is probably more an indication of the astuteness of the winemaker and perhaps a little judicious blending.

The western ridge of the Santa Clara Valley is also region II vineyard area and has produced Cabernets which are different in style, but every bit the equal of Napa Cabernets. Production, unfortunately, is very limited.

The region II belt which crosses the Alexander Valley has also produced some fine Cabernets. There are some newly planted vineyards here and in other areas which have just recently come into bearing and will need time to be properly assessed. Among these are vineyards in the environs of the city of Ukiah in Mendocino County. Technically, this area is classed as region III, but there are valley and hillside areas which shade off into region II.

The fate of Cabernet Sauvignon in region II of Monterey County is difficult to assess at the moment. One can virtually write-off the strictly commercial ventures in this area, as far as Cabernet Sauvignon is concerned. This leaves Mirassou Vineyards which has produced some curious, very individual Cabernets. There are new region II plantings deep in the Carmel Valley which are just entering production and would bear careful attention.

The center of great Cabernet production in California seems to be in and around the tiny village of Rutherford in Napa Valley. Rutherford has become virtually synonymous with Beaulieu Vineyards. Let us take a couple of these fine Beaulieu Cabernets (made by Andre Tchelistcheff) as our point of departure.

Beaulieu Cabernet Sauvignon, Private Reserve, 1968

tasted at six years old

Huge, opulent, buttery Cabernet Sauvignon nose, just packed with fruit—particularly intense "black currant" character typical of Cabernet, especially in California. Very full on the palate, fine sugar/acid balance with some residual tannin. Nicely ready but will develop further for a few years. A very elegant wine. This is a classic California Cabernet Sauvignon. This wine is so packed with fruit that it is virtually beyond comparison with *any* Bordeaux. There is a fair amount of (American) oak in the wine, but the fruit just pushes the wood right into the background. In so many respects, this wine *is* Napa Valley Cabernet Sauvignon.

Beaulieu Cabernet Sauvignon, Private Reserve, 1965

tasted at eight years old

This wine is somewhat darker than the 1968—very deep color, almost a dark antique mahogany. Rich, overwhelming bouquet, tremendous fruit, plummy, slightly *"rôti"* (not in any pejorative sense); a distinct Napa *goût de terroir*—old timers in the valley refer to this as "Rutherford dust". A very complex nose. On the palate, a huge mouthful of wine, packed with grape essences. Unmistakably Napa in character. Huge, intense and yet beautifully balanced. There is the smile of a warm summer in this Cabernet.

The 1965 compares with the 1968 as, say, a 1964 Petrus compares with a 1966 Margaux.

This 1965 Cabernet was a superb accompaniment to a very simply prepared roast duckling—the insides were rubbed with salt and freshly ground pepper and the cavity was stuffed with a few sprigs of fresh thyme. The roasting completed, a simple pan gravy was made with the addition of rich stock and a touch of Madeira.

Beaulieu Cabernets are 100% Cabernet Sauvignon. This is a major departure from the general practice in the Medoc (Bordeaux) where several different varieties (e.g., Petit Verdot, Malbec and Merlot) are used to blend into the Cabernet. In the Pomerol district of Bordeaux; Merlot, rather than Cabernet, is the predominant grape variety while in the St. Emilion district the variety Cabernet Franc is the most widely planted.

The first significant plantings of Cabernet Sauvignon in California in the late 19th century were generally accompanied by some blending varieties in the manner identical to Medoc vineyards. It seems that as Cabernet Sauvignon gained ascendancy in California many of these other vines were grafted over to Cabernet.

In recent years, the question of the 100% Cabernet vs. the Cabernet blend has been reopened. There has been a great deal of controversy over the question whether the Bordeaux practice of blending a softer, more quickly maturing variety into Cabernet is appropriate in California. Several influential voices have been raised strongly advising the use of Merlot as a blending variety. The 1965 and 1968 Beaulieu Cabernet masterpieces of Andre Tchelistcheff certainly argue for the preferability of 100% Cabernet Sauvignon. It is interesting to note that during the 1940's the Beaulieu estate had plantings of Petit Verdot, Malbec and Merlot. According to Tchelistcheff, the Malbec vines produced a neutral wine which seemed to contribute nothing to the finished wine. Malbec is being used less and less in Bordeaux and is not used for blending in any of the First Great Growths. Petit Verdot is blended into Chateau Lafite at about 15%. There were problems with Petit Verdot on the Beaulieu estate in that it did not ripen to Tchelistcheff's satisfaction. He found that the Merlot precipitated the maturation process too rapidly for what he believed to be the proper development of *his* Cabernet. Certainly seven to ten years is not too long to wait for a Beaulieu Cabernet, judging by the rewards which this patience pays.

Several other winemakers use blends of one sort or another—Merlot being the most widely used. It is most interesting to compare these with the 100% Cabernets. Inglenook Special Cask Cabernet uses approximately 15% Merlot while the regular bottling is a 100% Cabernet. Freemark Abbey uses Merlot at approximately 10% as do Chappellet and Sterling Vineyards. The following notes might be enlightening.

Freemark Abbey Cabernet Sauvignon, 1968

tasted at five years old

Quite fully developed at this age. Immensely fruity Cabernet, good residual sugar brings out the fruit, making this a nice "fat" wine with just enough acidity to hold it together with none to spare. Low in residual tannins. I tasted this against a five year old Sutter Home Zinfandel (Deaver Ranch, Amador County). The Cabernet had only slightly more "stuffing" than the Zinfandel. Both were immensely pleasant to drink, but the Freemark Abbey lacked the complexity that one seeks in a Cabernet Sauvignon. The fact that it was made from eight year old vines may have had something to do with the lack of complexity.

Inglenook Cabernet Sauvignon, Special Cask, 1968

tasted at five and one half years old, 15% merlot blend

Certainly one of the loveliest Inglenook wines in memory. I had heard several disparaging remarks about this wine so that my surprise was most pleasant. Deep, clear, garnet red. Absolutely lovely, complex nose, very much like a fairly light weight St. Julien—say a 1967 Léoville Poyferré. On the palate, lighter, less mouth-filling than one would have suspected from the bouquet. Nevertheless, very satisfying at this point but definitely not a wine to hold onto for very long. An elegant wine to serve with sautéed milk-fed veal chops, garnished with medallions of herb and lemon butter.

Inglenook Cabernet Sauvignon, Special Cask, 1965

tasted at seven years old, 15% merlot blend

Much darker than the 1968, slightly brick red at the edges. A marvelous, big, berry-cabernet nose, just slightly *"rôti"*. Very elegant nose. But the bouquet was curiously disconnected from the wine on the palate—an almost disembodied bouquet! Very light on the palate, lacking the intensity which the bouquet seemed to indicate. A weak, almost vanishing finish. Obviously very weak in fixed acidity. What a tragedy!

Inglenook Cabernet Sauvignon, (regular bottling), 1965

tasted at seven and one half years old, 100% cabernet

A dark, handsome wine; on the nose, immense fruit, berry-cabernet. On the palate, soft, velvety, well bred, lots of "stuffing"; considerable residual tannin and a fine, long finish. Nicely matched in this tasting with grilled spring lamb. There was enough of the wine left in the decanter to finish off with a nice French Double Crème. Against the cheese, the residual sugars came to the fore and the wine took on a darker, richer, more plummy character, standing up beautifully to the cheese. Although I had tasted bottles of this wine before and have tasted it since, the wine seemed to be at its peak for this tasting.

Of course, this is not a fair sampling from which to draw any definitive conclusions. Yet the fact remains that at least in some Cabernet-Merlot blends, there is a tendency toward "bottoming out", lacking finish. In some cases, at least, the addition of Merlot reduces fixed acidity and, finally, aging potential.

There are two things which should be considered: first, a special peculiarity of the Cabernet Sauvignon grape; and second, some fundamental environmental differences between California and Bordeaux.

With regard to Cabernet Sauvignon as a variety, important experiments at the University of California, Davis, have confirmed the fact that there seems not to be a very great difference in Cabernet grown in the cool end of region II (at 2501 degree days) and the warm end (3000 degree days). In either temperature regimen, Cabernet is a very late ripening grape. The typical picking date for Cabernet is the middle of October. Acidity respires from the grape berry at a more rapid rate under conditions of greater warmth during the ripening period. In California, the slow final ripening of Cabernet under the cooler October weather conditions, gives the Cabernet grape the opportunity to retain much better total acidity. Merlot ripens some three to four weeks earlier under considerably warmer conditions. Although the heat summation for the entire growing season is similar to Bordeaux, the September heat summation is considerably higher in California than it is in Bordeaux. There are two reasons for this: first, being farther south, the day is longer to a degree that makes a significant temperature difference; and second, the interior valleys are significantly cooler in September, thus lessening the effectiveness of the Bay Area natural air conditioning system. Whereas the Cabernet has just the right balancing acidity; the Merlot, ripening under warm September conditions, is often deficient in acidity. Apparently, the blend throws off the acid balance of the Cabernet. In Bordeaux, the situation with regard to Cabernet is not as ideal as it is in California. There is a far greater chance of late September, early October rains in the Medoc than there is in Napa. Consequently, there is a far greater danger in leaving Cabernet on the vines to ripen as fully as it does in California, and it is generally picked at a slightly lower degree brix and a considerably higher total acidity. A "green" Bordeaux is not entirely uncommon, but a "green" California Cabernet is virtually unheard of. The blending of some Merlot or other early ripener, is virtually essential in Bordeaux.

That this might well be the case, let us take a further look at some 100% California Cabernets.

Mayacamas Cabernet Sauvignon, 1965, Napa

tasted at nine years old

Chateau Branaire du Cru, 1966, Bordeaux, St. Julien

tasted at eight years old

I had selected the Mayacamas to accompany an English style roast prime rib and Yorkshire pudding dinner. As I decanted the Mayacamas, a wisp of bouquet reached my nose and the thought flashed across my mind—"Branaire du Cru 1966!". The decanting was carefully completed and I went to the cellar, cradled and decanted a personal favorite, St. Julien, Branaire '66. I do not generally encourage wine conversation unless the guests are dedicated wine connoisseurs; but, in this case, the contrast of the wines was so fascinating that it usurped a good part of the dinner conversation.

The two wines were absolutely identical to the eye, somewhere between dark ruby and dark mahogany. Both had a remarkable grassy-organic nose, typical of some Clarets, of equal intensity and at first virtually indistinguishable. One might compare the nose to the smell of a new-mown hay field. The Branaire was ever so slightly more austere, more acidic, while the Mayacamas wore a bit more of a smile, ever so slightly softer.

Both were absolutely first-rate Clarets on the palate, the organic flavors carried through beautifully. The Branaire was still somewhat more austere, some residual sugars but a somewhat insistent acidity which kept the flavors alive on the palate. The Mayacamas had excellent but somewhat less insistent acidity and somewhat more attractive residual sweetness; less spread out over the palate, less mouthfilling, but the trace of sweetness came forward to give a foundation to the superb fruit of the wine.

As the wines developed in glass and decanter, the Mayacamas bouquet showed more of a black-currant, berry character underlying the basic organic flavors; the berry character became richer as the wine opened up. The bouquet of the Branaire became somewhat floral with a very slight berry background.

One of the most remarkable things about the two wines was that one could not discern any differences which could be assigned to the *goût de terroir* of the two vineyards.

Perhaps even more remarkable is the fact that the Mayacamas is a 100% Cabernet Sauvignon while the Branaire is a blend of 70% Cabernet Sauvignon with 30% Merlot. The Mayacamas was aged in American oak; whereas the Branaire was aged in new Yugoslav oak. In both cases, the oak was very much in the background. The guests flatly refused to vote a preference, so much did they enjoy the two wines!

Souverain Cellars Cabernet Sauvignon, 1962, Napa

tasted at ten years old

Lovely, dark, brilliant, slightly faded ruby. On the nose, a marvelous, rich bouquet—the kind of nose which Hugh Johnson calls the "cigar box aroma". An utterly classic Claret bouquet. On the palate, lots of fruit and an excellent acidity. Lots of "stuffing"—the wine was slightly burly and at the same time refined and elegant. One of the most perfectly balanced wines in memory. Right up there in the league of the First Great Growths.

Gemello's Cabernet Sauvignon, 1968, Santa Clara Valley (Lot 1)

tasted at seven and a half years old

Very deep, dark ruby with only the slightest hint of tawny at the edge of the glass. Evidently, the wine is just beginning to come into its prime.

Immensely fruity Cabernet nose. One thinks immediately of a big, important Puillac; but the wine is too big, too full-bodied for Bordeaux. This is California Cabernet at its best. There is a nice edge of Nevers oak, but this is well integrated into the fruit. The wine is developing a characteristic "cedar" nose (some Californians use the term "eucalyptus" to describe what is roughly the same characteristic). But the immensely fragrant, black currant fruitiness of the 100% Cabernet has the upper hand.

Like other big California Cabernets, there is excellent acidity but the big, mouthfilling character of the wine seems to derive more from the rich, black currant fruitiness and exceptional body (13.5% alcohol) of the wine, rather than subtle and delicate flavors which are underlined by higher acidity.

This is a trencherman's Cabernet, made for a superb, roasted rib of corn fed, midwest beef.

Charles Krug Cabernet Sauvignon-Vintage Selection 1965, Napa

tasted at ten years old

This is one of those fine, beautifully constructed Cabernets which start their lives as very hard, disagreeably tannic and "dusty" wines and then develop quite magnificently with a great deal of bottle age. The "dusty" character is not uncommon in developing Cabernets, particularly in California and to a lesser extent in Bordeaux. The effect is more like vacuum cleaner dust than a dustiness which one associates with the earth. It occurs quite naturally in big, undeveloped wines which have a great deal of extract and tannin and should not be confused with earthiness or oxydation. It tones down and finally fades with age.

This Krug Cabernet took about nine years to lose its tannic, "dusty" character, but what a wine underneath all that tannin!

Dark, antique mahogany in color. On the nose, there is still a trace of dustiness but the fruit has come up very beautifully. There is something of the "cedar" nose which occurs in the finest Cabernets. This "cedar" characteristic is probably the result of a complex marrying of fruit and oak aromas. The slight dustiness and the "cedar" character keep the intense fruit in balance.

Quite dry, superbly balanced and elegant in the mouth—very much in the manner of a first growth Medoc. But the acidity is softer and the fruit runs deeper. This is a classic Napa Cabernet.

Whereas the fruit of Tchelistcheffs Beaulieu Cabernets comes on very boldly, here the fruit is subdued and intense. A very subtle trace of Napa earth gives a nice emphasis to the fruit, both on the nose and on the palate. There is a great deal of "breed" to this wine. An important and eminently satisfying Cabernet.

This is one of the few California Cabernets which call for very elegant, Bordelaise style cuisine.

These are only a few of an extraordinary assortment of Cabernet Sauvignon (blended and unblended) which have been made and are being made in California. Some of the best of these are still very much in their ascendency: the extraordinary Heitz-Martha's Vineyard Cabernets, other more recent Cabernets of Mayacamas and Souverain Cellars, superb cabernets of Oakville Vineyards, Ridge, Chappellet, Clos du Val, Stag's Leap Wine Cellars, to mention only a few. Several of these wines seem to be on their way to vindicating those who have advocated the use of Merlot, particularly the magnificent Chappellet Cabernet 1970. The mountain growing conditions at Chappellet seem to produce a blending Merlot which adds a certain opulent complexity to the wine rather than simple fruitiness. Far from hindering the development of the wine, this particular blend has produced a wine which is likely to go on improving for several years.

Other winemakers are getting a better feeling for Merlot and are learning to control it appropriately as a blending wine. We have very little evidence at this point to make any final judgments. This much can be said, however: both Cabernet and Merlot behave rather differently in California than they do in Bordeaux.

In California, there are extensive new vineyards planted to Merlot which are just beginning to come into production. By a curious irony, these extensive plantings might well turn out to be one of the most fortuitous gambles made by California vignerons. Judging from most recent vintages, there seems to be a gradual cooling trend occurring in the climate of California (whether this is a permanent or a temporary phenomenon is a matter of considerable controversy). It will be most interesting to watch how Merlot behaves in these more recent cooler vintage years.

We have had an interesting varietal bottling of Merlot by Louis Martini which, in spite of its awkward beginning, has turned out to be a very pleasant wine.

Louis Martini Merlot 1971

tasted at four years old

Good dark but slightly dull ruby. On the nose, intriguingly reminiscent of a lesser Pomerol. There is a rather simple, mellow fruitiness with an unusual wood background (redwood vats and then finished briefly in American oak?). Nicely mellow and fruity on the palate with adequate acidity. A rather provincial, countrified version of a Pomerol but certainly a nice, useful wine for the price.

The wine was especially good served with a fricassee of fresh rabbit. The rabbit was cut up, sautéed in butter and then braised with plenty of fresh herbs, white onions, mushrooms, garlic, stock and a splash of the Merlot.

Far more interesting is this:

Sterling Vineyards Cabernet Sauvignon (with Merlot), a non-vintage, Napa Wine, a marriage of 1970–1971

tasted, summer, 1975

This is not a "grand" wine nor was it intended to be one. There is a nice dark ruby tone to the appearance. How immensely agreeable on the nose! There is the rich black currant aroma with slight grassy overtones which one associates with Cabernet but there is also the mellow, rather simple fruit fragrance of Merlot. The wine is evidently quite ready to drink at this point.

On the palate there is stuffing and complexity but there is a nice fruitiness backed up by some wood which makes this wine, not only agreeable but remarkably stylish. The wine is immensely pleasing in addition to being priced significantly below many big 100% Cabernets; the wine does not put one through the agonizing discipline of cellar aging. One has no moral scruples about robbing the cradle as far as *this* wine is concerned! And yet it has style and elegance. The use of Merlot seems to be completely controlled and the wine realizes the intention of the winemaker (Ric Forman) quite beautifully.

Here is a nice wine for Fillet of Beef Marchand de Vin or perhaps a fine sautéed minute steak with shallots. A wine of this caliber obviously fills a major vacuum in the line-up of California's Claret type wines, bridging the gap between the big 100% Cabernets and the more coarsely textured Zinfandels made in the style of Claret.

   We have had some other lighter, less costly Cabernets and Cabernet/Merlot blends which fit in here. Most notably, there have been some very nice Cabernets from Pedroncelli and Kenwood and, *mirable dictu*, a superb jug Cabernet from Italian Swiss Colony!

California Pinot Noir

Eight

In a report on wine grape varieties made by the University of California in 1896, Professor E. W. Hilgard wrote: "In some localities it is doubtless possible to make Pinot Noir wine of high quality and to age it, but only with a minute attention to detail and an elaborate care, which no price that is likely to be obtained at present would justify."

Pinot Noir is unquestionably the most difficult vine to cultivate and the one which offers the greatest challenge to the art of the winemaker. If this is true of the French Pinot Noir of the Burgundy region, it is even more true of California Pinot Noir. Tchelistcheff is reported to have said, "Pinot Noir is scrawny and broods about the slightest offense. All the challenge is in getting the surly child to smile."

The classic Burgundian version of Pinot Noir is generally strung between an excellent acidity and appropriately fine residual sugars. Within this frame, there are fruit flavors, oak, and the uncanny ability to develop extraordinary bottle complexity. The whole effect of the wine is one of silkiness and great richness. While a Burgundian Pinot Noir can be a big, hearty wine (living up to its image) it can also come off as a very delicate, intensely flavored wine. It is interesting to note that the bigger, heartier French Pinot Noirs generally come from the more *northerly* Côte de Nuits, while the more delicate version generally comes from the more *southerly* Côte de Beaune. There are some Pinot Noir vineyards which are even further to the south, near the towns of Mercury and Givry, along the Côte Chalonnaise, between the Côte d'Or and the Beaujolais regions. These are by far the lightest French Pinot Noirs, light both in character and in pigmentation. In addition, the quality of the wines is far more erratic than Côte d'Or Pinot Noirs.

These more southerly vineyards bear the closest resemblance to conditions in California and, as one might expect, California Pinot Noirs are more reminiscent of the wines of the Chalonnaise than they are of the more classic Pinot Noirs of the Côte d'Or. They also seem to have the same problem with widely divergent levels of quality. One vintage might be superb and the next will be very ordinary.

In fact, California Pinot Noirs will very often be light weight to the point of being thin, poorly pigmented, and awkward. But occasionally one will find a California Pinot Noir of exceptional quality and one's faith is restored.

The finest Burgundian Pinot Noirs are grown on the "Golden Slope", the Côte d'Or. The slope is a rather abrupt end of a plateau rather than the side of a valley. The early morning sun sweeps across the plain to warm the vineyards and give them the golden glow for which the slope is named. The eastern exposure protects the vines from the extreme of mid-day overhead sun. The soils are particularly effective in retaining heat, once the sun has gone beyond the slope. Temperatures are very constant; there are few radical swings.

Normally, Pinot Noir ripens in mid-September, when the temperature is quite cool in Burgundy. The mean daytime and nightime temperature is often only a few degrees above 50°. It is often necessary to add sugar to the must (a practice which is forbidden by law in California).

In California, the temperature during the September ripening period is considerably higher, for reasons which we discussed in the previous chapter. The sugar/acid balance of the great Burgundies is lost in the heat. To compound the problem, the vines, which require a great deal of pampering, have suffered neglect because the poorer California version of the wine could not command sufficiently high prices to warrant the attention which they demand. By the 1960's, many of the vines had degenerated considerably. The university set about to clean out the off-strains which had developed and to select the healthier, purer strains for propagation. In all, there are over fifty strains or "clones" of Pinot Noir.[1] One of the major

---

[1] The variety "Gamay Beaujolais", which is widely planted in California, is not a true Gamay, but is one of the clones of Pinot Noir.

problems is to select the clone which is most suitable for the micro-climate of a particular vineyard. The process of careful clonal selection has been going on since the university first began its research. We are only beginning to see the results.

Normally, California Pinot Noirs are relatively low in acid and are lightly pigmented. In an attempt to come up with a Pinot Noir which more closely resembles the robust wines of the Côte de Nuits, many California winemakers have traditionally blended in some Petite Sirah to make up for some of the lack of pigmentation. The variety Petite Sirah generally develops very deep coloration. But to my taste, this practice is only occasionally successful. The strong Petite Sirah flavors cover the delicate fruit of the Pinot Noir. The two varieties mature in bottle at different rates, never becoming totally integrated. The result is more like a Côtes du Rhône in an off year.

A major exception was a superb Pinot Noir of Sebastiani (Sonoma).

Sebastiani Pinot Noir, Bin #121, Sonoma

Special bottling for Esquin Imports (San Francisco wine merchants)

tasted at seven years old

Although it was not stated on the label, most of this wine was from vintage 1964. The grapes were picked at unusually high brix and high acid readings. There was some Petite Sirah blended into the wine, which was then matured in a huge redwood vat.

The wine looks very much like a Côte de Nuits Burgundy; somewhat brick red at the edges; very bright, with lots of sheen. On the nose, a peacock's tail of a bouquet blooms immediately; considerable Pinot Noir character, reminiscent of a Côte de Nuits, yet the unmistakable *goût de terroir* of California; a big wine with lots of fruit (I was reminded of pomegranate and a hint of something like carmelized sugar—somewhat different from the *"rôti"* character); again, a very complex nose. On the palate, rich and appetizing, excellent sugar/acid balance with all the aromatic characteristics coming across on the palate. A shade shorter on the finish than a Côte de Nuits. A major success.

Charles Krug, Louis Martini and, formerly, Wente Brothers, have traditionally made their Pinot Noirs with some Petite Sirah blended in. These wines take a few years to come up to their full potential and can be very nice Rhône-type wines. The 1967 Charles Krug Pinot Noir (special vintage selection) is certainly the finest of the Krug Pinot Noirs. Sonoma Vineyards has given us some surprisingly nice, stylish Pinot Noirs in this manner, from grapes grown in their Russian River vineyards (region I). The Petite Sirah from this area is much lighter, less insistent than Petite Sirah grown in the Napa Valley; consequently, it marries more agreeably with the Pinot Noir.

Another school of thought holds that a Pinot Noir should be 100% of that variety, that any blending throws off the delicate fruit which is characteristic of Pinot Noir. In this version, the vines are carefully pruned so that the fruit comes on big; no attempt is made to ferment to bone-dryness; and the winemaker does not worry too much about the lack of pigmentation. The wine is then aged in small Limousin oak barrels.

Freemark Abbey Pinot Noir, 1969, Napa

tasted at five years old

Freemark Abbey chooses this latter school of thought and it shows in the fine quality of the wine. Very lightly pigmented, pale to the extent that it is a shade off the color of a rosé. But the sheen and luminosity of the wine tells one that this is no rosé. A rather simple but nice, full Pinot Noir bouquet, lacking complexity but still very attractive. A nice fat wine on the palate, loaded with fruit extract and an appropriate residual sweetness. The wine reminds one of succulent tree-ripened fruit. This is a superb wine for California's excellent "Rouge et Noir" brand soft-ripening cheeses.

Certainly one of the finest California Pinot Noirs made in this manner was:

Hanzell Pinot Noir, 1966, Sonoma

tasted at seven years old

An intense, silky red; a very handsome wine to look at. On the nose, something related to—but quite different from—the classic Pinot Noir fragrance. A much darker, more exotic aroma;

perhaps at harvest some of the berries had shriveled to raisins; a hint of old vintage Port; just the right amount of oak; immediate realization that only the finest new French Limousin oak cooperage was used. On the palate, a very soft, well bred, civilized wine, obviously the product of a master winemaker (Brad Webb); a wine which calls for rich, well-marbled, prime grade American beef.

This has remained, for me, the most memorable of the Hanzell Pinot Noirs, although subsequent vintages have maintained a level of excellence unusual for California Pinot Noir.

Charles Wagner, a grower who for years sold fine Pinot Noir grapes to various Napa wineries, now has his own small winery—Caymus Vineyards. The 1972 vintage Pinot Noir from Caymus is 100% of the variety and is aged in Limousin oak. I tasted a small, *unfiltered* lot of this 1972 Pinot Noir and I must say that it was the most elegant Napa Pinot Noir in memory. Most of the wine which came on the market was given a light filtering. Although it is fine Pinot Noir, it seems to have suffered from this processing. Perhaps a year or two additional bottle age will prove me wrong. It is, after all, notoriously difficult to predict the future of a young Pinot Noir. At any rate, I believe that we can expect some of the finest California Pinot Noirs of the future to come from Caymus Vineyards.

Some very nice Pinot Noirs have come from the region I Carneros district of Napa, including some successful, unblended Pinot Noirs made at Z-D Winery (Sonoma). The 1972 Z-D Pinot Noir promises to develop into a splendid wine.

Perhaps the most extraordinary Pinot Noir to come from the Carneros District was this:

Beaulieu Pinot Noir, 1968, Napa

tasted at five and one half years old

Huge bouquet and a great mouthful of wine—so impressive, so perfectly balanced, so completely together, that it rather defies analysis. A very dark, bright wine (looks more like a Pomerol than a Burgundy). A beautifully perfumed wine, not comparable to a Côte d'Or wine, rather in a class by itself; the Pinot character is very dark, very ripe. This is unmistakably a Napa Valley wine, smelling of volcanic soil and perfectly ripened fruit. Rather heady like a Rhône. Good acid and tremendous fruitiness on the nose and on the palate—reminiscent of prunes which have been steeped in wine. A strong, excellent finish. One of Andre Tchelistcheff's masterpieces.

Joe Heitz made a fairly big Napa Pinot Noir in 1968. By its fifth year this wine had bloomed into a remarkably "plummy" Pinot Noir (one will occasionally run across a very plummy Côte d'Or Burgundy)—a charming wine with an immediate appeal; packed with fruit, but somehow one dimensional, lacking in depth and elegance.

A less obvious, but more classic Pinot Noir was made at Sterling Vineyards (Napa) in 1971. In a recent tasting, this wine had that curious dark aroma which reminds me of cocoa and freshly roasted coffee beans (most likely the result of a complex marriage of fruit and wood). It is not unusual to find this very distinct aroma in fine Côte d'Or Burgundies. Unlike so many California Pinot Noirs which fail miserably on the palate, this wine has a nice flow and balance on its way across the palate; a wine to complement a good ripe French Brie.

A really delightful Pinot Noir, very much in the manner of a Givry, was made at Carneros Creek Winery in 1973. It certainly makes much more sense to produce a light, stylish, early maturing Pinot Noir such as this 1973 Carneros Creek, rather than trying to make a big, Côte de Nuits style Pinot Noir, except when there are unusually ideal weather conditions. An even finer Pinot Noir was made in this lighter style at Stonegate Winery (Napa) in 1973.

There have been some interesting Pinot Noirs made in areas other than Napa/Sonoma. To the north, a surprisingly fine series of Pinot Noirs has been made at Parducci (Ukiah). Perhaps the more northerly situation of the vineyards is a contributing factor. All the emphasis, in the Parducci version, is on the pure fruit of the Pinot Noir. There is only a slight trace of redwood character in the wine. As appealing as these wines can be, they lack the complexity for which one looks in Pinot Noir.

The 1970 and 1971 vintage Pinot Noirs made at Pedroncelli from vineyards up in the rolling hills above the western rim of the Alexander Valley, have been fairly big wines aged in *Nevers* oak. Tasted at three years old, the wines were very attractive but the Bordelais oak character, so appropriate for Cabernet Sauvignon, seemed to overwhelm the subtlety of the fruit. The wines were monochromatic in effect. But in more recent tastings the wines are developing a great deal of complexity and finesse, superior to several highly touted Pinot Noirs priced three and four times higher.

To the south, Max Heubner at Mirassou has made some exceptional Pinot Noir from grapes grown in the Salinas Valley, Monterey County. The 1966 and 1969 Harvest Selection Pinot Noirs were subtle, well balanced wines which straddled the line between fruitiness which lacks complexity and the use of oak which overwhelms the fruit. By its fifth year, the 1966 Pinot Noir had developed into a fairly light, stylish wine with subtle depths of flavor and a remarkable sugar/acid balance, reminiscent of a fine Santenay. The 1969 was a bigger wine with a lovely perfumed, almost spicy, bouquet.

In 1974, Mario Gemello (Gemello Winery, Santa Clara) made a very successful Burgundian style wine from a new and improved Gamay. Beaujolais clone (Stonegate Pinot Noir is made from this same clone). The grapes were from a new vineyard deep in the Carmel Valley, south of Monterey. The wine is very carefully made with lots of French oak; not a very complex wine but fruity, fragrant and consistently pleasing.

There are other interesting Pinot Noirs made in the Santa Clara Valley and Monterey County areas; but the quantities are so limited, often the price is so prohibitively high, and the wines are so difficult to hunt down that it is not really fair to take them into consideration.

California Zinfandel

Nine

There are several current hypotheses on the origin of Zinfandel. According to one account, it has its origin in a cutting which Agoston Haraszthy brought back from Europe in 1862. Unfortunately, the marking on the identification tag was almost completely illegible. The name "Zinfandel" was the nearest that could be made out of the scrawl.

More recent evidence has indicated that the appearance of Zinfandel in California might have ante-dated Haraszthy's European trip by several years. There are indications that the Zinfandel, known by another name, is a blending variety grown in southern Italy. Zinfandel does reasonably well in the warmer regions III and IV (comparable to Sicily). This is a possible corroborating argument for its more southerly origin.

Whether or not Agoston Haraszthy actually discovered and introduced Zinfandel into California is a matter of some controversy. On the other hand, he was most certainly one of the first to understand its merits as a grape variety well suited to California and was instrumental in promoting its popularity. Haraszthy also initiated the practice of aging Zinfandel in large redwood vats.

Zinfandel became a particular favorite of the many Italians who settled in California. Italian winemakers utilized Zinfandel for making an old world style everyday wine. But Zinfandel also lent itself to more careful treatment. It could be made into a lighter, more complex wine which vaguely resembled French Claret. And during the early years, Zinfandel was also used to make a *"blanc de noir"* type of white wine.

By the year 1880, Zinfandel and the original Mission grape variety which the Spanish padres had introduced were the two most widely planted varieties in California.

Unfortunately, one of the problems with Zinfandel is that its vines can be heavily over-cropped, resulting in a very low-grade, "rot-gut" type wine. As the demand for California wine increased, growers succumbed to the temptation of over-cropping Zinfandel vines to meet demand. By the late

1880's Zinfandel had developed a very bad reputation and other French and Italian premium varietals became more widely planted.

But there was still much to recommend about Zinfandel. Italian winemakers continued to make Zinfandel and store it in large redwood casks, drinking it up well within two years of each vintage. Young Zinfandel made in this manner was very much reminiscent of the wine which they had enjoyed in the old country. And the young wine, zesty with fruit acidity, went well with Italian food. A good current example of a Zinfandel made in this manner would be the non-vintage Zinfandel of Foppiano Vineyards (Healdsburg, Sonoma County).

Zinfandel made a decent enough wine practically anywhere it was grown in California. Because it was versatile, highly productive and did not require a great deal of attention, Zinfandel had been used extensively in the production of bulk wines.

But familiarity bred contempt. Because of its reputation as an everyday beverage wine, it was assumed that it was capable of nothing higher. Zinfandel was much maligned in wine literature and in the attitude of the wine buying public.

Following Prohibition, Louis Martini in Napa, the Parduccis in Ukiah, and Frank Bartholomew at Buena Vista (Sonoma) were the first to rediscover and explore the higher possibilities of Zinfandel. They maintained the traditional methods but carefully pruned back the vines to reduce productivity and then made the wine with great care, treating Zinfandel as a premium varietal. They made an outstanding series of Zinfandels during the 1960's. In the late 1960's, Lee Stewart, Mario Gemello, and others, experimented with the use of fine French oak cooperage for aging fine Zinfandel.

In 1965, Charles Myers, a teacher at Sacramento City College and amateur winemaker, made Zinfandel from some very old vines in the

Shenandoah Valley (Amador County) located up in the foothills of the Sierras just east of Sacramento. The results were far beyond his expectations and he subsequently got Darrell Corti of Corti Brothers, Sacramento, interested in the area. Through Darrell, Bob Trinchero of Sutter Home Winery (Napa Valley) became interested and produced the first of his very fine Zinfandels from Amador grapes in 1968. Myers has since opened his own small Harbor Winery in west Sacramento.

In the Santa Clara Valley, Dave Bennion and Paul Draper at Ridge Vineyards and Dr. David Bruce were exploring some of the possibilities of Zinfandel. Experiments were made with late picked Zinfandel grapes and some extraordinary wines were made. A white wine was made from the free run juice of Zinfandel (in the same manner that "white" champagne is made from Pinot Noir) with interesting results.

Wine drinkers were discovering that a well made Zinfandel has remarkable and unsuspected aging potential. Old bottles, tucked away in some forgotten corner of a wine cellar were turning up, and to the surprise of many, not only had great staying power, but had developed remarkable bottle bouquet.

The possibilities still seem endless as each new vintage turns up some unsuspectedly fine result. Zinfandel has become the most versatile, the most useful and one of the most interesting wine grapes grown in California.

It is difficult to get a handle on the basic characteristics of Zinfandel since, depending up on how it is made, it can appear in remarkably different guises. I have drunk Zinfandel which in a blind tasting I would have identified as a fresh, young Beaujolais. Others have been reminiscent of fine Italian wines such as Chianti, Barolo and Valpolicella. I have tasted Zinfandel which compares to all but the highest level of Bordeaux wine. Recently a fine Zinfandel (1969 Zinfandel of Joseph Swan Vineyards,

Sonoma County) was slipped into a blind tasting of a range of fine Bordeaux and was almost unanimously acclaimed to be one of the finest Medocs on the table!

Unlike many other grape varieties grown in California, Zinfandel retains excellent acidity when grown in north coast vineyards. It ripens anywhere from the middle of September until late October, depending upon the vintage. It has perhaps a better chance of having good sugar/acid balance than any other red grape variety grown in California. Zinfandel has the curious habit of ripening unevenly: some grape clusters will be partially turned to raisins; while other clusters will be just barely ripe. Zinfandel often develops what is called a "second crop". These are small, late developing clusters which are still unripe well into the middle of October. Perhaps this curious habit of uneven ripening is one of the reasons for the good sugar/acid balance characteristic of Zinfandel.

If there is any one varietal characteristic, it is an aroma which is reminiscent of fresh red raspberries or occasionally of black raspberries. In certain Zinfandels at a particular stage of development, this raspberry aroma can be uncanny and unmistakable. One of the finest Zinfandels I have ever tasted was a huge, fleshy three year old Napa wine which was redolent with the aroma and flavor of freshly crushed, superbly ripe, black raspberries. Lighter Zinfandels can be remarkably red raspberry-like, sprightly and appetizing.

The berry fruitiness of young Zinfandel can be so assertive, so attractive, that one can lose sight of the acidity, the residual sugars, and the tannin underneath which gives it its aging potential. Understandably, the tendency is to drink it all up while it is young. But a small investment and a modicum of patience can yield a great deal of wine drinking pleasure.

In my own experience, I have found that as Zinfandel settles down in the bottle it often goes through a very awkward stage as its big, fresh fruit character tones down. I have had Zinfandels which were beautifully fresh and berry-like only a month or two in the bottle. A year later I found them listless and off-tasting with a disagreeable bitter finish. If this is the case, one should not assume that the wine is over the hill. The thing to do is put it away for a couple of years and let it settle down. This latter characteristic makes Zinfandel somewhat difficult to judge properly. In a comparison tasting, a very fine Zinfandel might show very poorly because it is going through this adjustment. However, if a Zinfandel is showing well as it leaves the cask, the chances are that it will come around nicely in a few years.

Perhaps the most classic example of a fine California Zinfandel is the one made by Louis Martini in 1968.

Louis Martini Zinfandel, 1968, a blend of Napa Valley Zinfandel and Zinfandel from Martini's Monte Rosso Vineyard, high in the Mayacamas Range

tasted at three years old

A nice bright red, not too darkly pigmented. On the nose, reminiscent of a Beaujolais, perhaps a Moulin-a-Vent. Some raspberry character. A lively, zesty wine on the palate, with sugar/acid/fruit balance very similar to a fine Beaujolais. And yet this is inimitably a California wine. *So* drinkable!

tasted at four years old

The wine has lost its bright, zesty quality. Somewhat thin and ragged on the palate, with a curious bitter aftertaste which is not exactly becoming.

tasted at five and one half years old

The delightful, racy mouthful of two and a half years ago has become a wine to ponder, to take seriously. The color is bright garnet, with lots of sheen and sparkle. Not immediately forthcoming on the nose, the wine has to come up in the glass. The fresh raspberry nose has become darker, more mature, slightly buttery. The difference between the youthful stage and the more mature stage of Zinfandel is similar to the difference between two vintage ports, one, say, five years old and the other fifteen years old; or perhaps the difference between fresh fruit and fruit preserves.

On the palate, the residual sugars come forward more distinctly, having lost its fresh fruit acidity. And yet the wine still has good sugar/acid balance. Some residual tannin which had passed unnoticed before is in evidence now. The wine does not have the authority of a Cabernet but it is still quite assertive. All traces of bitterness have disappeared. This is a rounded, supple wine of superb quality. The remarkable fact is that one would hardly have suspected that a wine of this importance was originally priced under $2.00 a bottle, it represents an exceptional value.

tasted at seven years old

The wine seems to be darker. The nose is now rich and forth-coming. It has developed some of those fruit and wood complexities which one finds in older Cabernets. The Zinfandel character is very dark and full, reminding one of very ripe fruit. There is something which indicates that the wine will have a nice sweet edge.

On the palate, richly fruity, rather like very ripe August fruits —plums, peaches and figs. Medium dry, full-bodied, plenty of residual sweetness balanced by good acid and, still, a noticeable residuum of tannin. At this stage the wine was splendid with roast duck and also stood up nicely to an assortment of cheeses, including mild cheddar.

I have selected this Louis Martini 1968 Zinfandel, not as a rare and exceptional wine, but rather as a prototype of the basically sturdy, well made, reasonably priced California Zinfandel. Fortunately, there is a reasonable abundance of these wines available. I am thinking, for example, of other Martini Zinfandels, as well as some of the Zinfandels of Sebastiani, Parducci, Pedroncelli, Barengo Cellars (Lodi), Mirassou, Ridge, Sonoma Vineyards, Fetzer, Souverain of Alexander Valley, as well as some Zinfandels made at the smaller, less publicized "country" wineries. Most of these Zinfandels are more fullbodied, perhaps coarser than the 1968 Martini, but they often represent the same exceptional value for money. A little sleuthing can turn up some superb wines at very reasonable prices. Perhaps at the top of this class of Zinfandels, and every bit as fine as the 1968 Martini, are the 1970 and 1971 Special Bin Zinfandels of Kenwood Vineyards, Sonoma.

Anyone who is developing even a modest wine cellar should give these wines a great deal of attention. At prices ranging from $1.50 to $3.00 per bottle, one can afford to lay some of these wines away. One's patience and investment will be richly rewarded, even though one might occasionally make a mistake. Provided that the wine is dry, with reasonably good acidity and depth of fruit, and perhaps some wood character (a judicious amount of redwood character in Zinfandel can be very attractive), many of these wines will benefit immeasurably from additional years of bottle age.

Lee Stewart's Souverain Zinfandels are quite different in style. His 1970 Zinfandel is certainly among the finest ever made in California.

Souverain Zinfandel, 1970, Napa

tasted at one and three quarters years old (two weeks in the bottle)

Very dark, black raspberry purple, bright and clean. On the nose, something reminiscent of butter-caramel giving way to the aroma of freshly crushed black raspberries. The fresh black raspberry carries right over onto the palate. Lovely to drink.

tasted at two and three quarters years old

Big Zinfandel character but noticeably and disagreeably bitter on the palate.

tasted at four years old

Very dark ruby, lots of glycerine. Rich berry/plummy Zinfandel nose. At first the nose is slightly peppery, but this gives way, as the wine opens up to a dark, aromatic character quite difficult to describe, but similar to that found in very big Côte de Nuits Burgundies. The wine spent over a year and a half in Nevers oak and although the Nevers character is easy to recognize, it is only a background character in the magnificent bouquet.

Medium-dry on the palate but with lots of balancing acidity. There are tastes which remind one by turns of very ripe plums, of blackberries, and of pomegranate. These intense fruit flavors linger very insistently on the palate. The oak keeps the wine from being too embarrassingly fruity. Any bitterness has disappeared completely; hidden underneath the fruit, there is considerable residual tannin.

One thinks vaguely of Pomerol, or again of big Côte de Nuits Burgundy or of superb Chianti Classico. But the wine, so redolent with the flavors of superbly ripe fruit, defies any comparison whatsoever. It is uniquely and inimitably a great California wine.

There is something about this Zinfandel that makes one think of ham. It has been an excellent accompaniment to a lightly cured ham baked in a pastry crust. It was also splendid served with roast goose this past Christmas.

Another fine Zinfandel, very much in the Italian style was:

Fetzer Vineyards Zinfandel, 1972, Ukiah, Mendocino County (a special lot from the ranches of Lolones and Stafford)

tasted at two years old

Valpolicella is known to most winelovers as a soft, friendly red wine from the Italian Veneto. While seldom what could be called first-rate or elegant, it is still a perfect accompaniment for the cuisine of the Veneto. Imagine, if you will, an ideal, exquisitely made, elegant Valpolicella and you will have some idea of what this Fetzer Zinfandel is like!

The wine is rather lightly pigmented and there is not much tannin but the fruit extract intensity runs very deep. There is less contrast between dark raisiny flavors and high fruit acid that one finds in some Zinfandel. The vines were cane-pruned on trellises so that there was more even ripening. In cane-pruning, the foliage acts as an umbrella, so that the fruit is not exposed to the direct rays of the sun, thus reducing the tendency to raisin. Rather than being fermented in large round vats, small, narrowly rectangular vats were used with the result that the must was fermented more evenly and at cooler temperature with greater fruit extraction and less tannin extraction.

On the nose, there is less raspberry and more of a spicy-peppery character. Fruit and subdued oak aromas play an interesting counterpoint.

The wine is quite dry, soft, with a lush texture of velvet, filling the mouth with flavor. The excellent acidity gives the wine a very special vigor, very much in the style of fine Italian wine.

This wine showed particularly well with a Breast of Chicken Parmigiano. The tomato sauce was made from home-grown, vine-ripened, fresh tomatoes. The trace of natural sugars and intense tomato flavor which came with vine ripening, showed through in the sauce and this served as a perfect complement to the wine.

Bob Trinchero at Sutter Home Winery in the Napa Valley has become somewhat of a Zinfandel specialist, thanks to some fine old Zinfandel vineyards in the foothills of the Sierras, southeast of Sacramento. His whole series of Zinfandels from these Amador County grapes has been of such uniformly high quality that they have become a staple in a good many fine wine cellars. The first of the series, made in 1968, is now in its prime.

Sutter Home Zinfandel, 1968, Lot 2, Deaver Ranch, Amador County

tasted at five and one half years old

This Zinfandel went through most of the problems which youthful Zinfandel goes through as it settles down. But thanks to the advice of my wine merchant, I mustered enough patience to leave my supply alone until it came around. This wine has a tremendous immediate appeal—it has been a great hit whenever I have served it.

A very dark ruby, just beginning to take on a tawny hue at the edge of the glass. An immensely rich, fruity nose; one thinks of plump Santa Clara prunes which have been steeped in a good Port. There is just enough oak to put some backbone into all that fruit. All these characteristics come right across on the palate; a medium-dry wine with a nice long finish. Very straightforward and luscious.

At an elaborate dinner in which more than one red wine is being served, this would be a perfect opening statement from which to step up to a big, complex California Cabernet.

All of these Zinfandels reflect very subtly the viticultural areas of their origin. The differences are virtually impossible to describe. One gradually develops a feeling for the special stamp which soil and micro-climate put on the wine. Since Zinfandel is grown in every important viticultural area in California, it is an excellent medium through which to develop a mental picture which charts these differences.

One of the best points of departure would be an exploration of the fine series of Zinfandels made at Ridge Vineyards from grapes grown in several different viticultural areas. These are not "rubber stamp" Zinfandels where everything remains more or less the same except the source of the grapes. Each Zinfandel from Ridge is made in a style eminently suited to the best which each lot of grapes has to offer.

In an interesting pair of Zinfandels from Gemello Winery, one can compare the effect which two different types of cooperage have on similar lots of Zinfandel.

Gemello Zinfandel, 1968–70 marriage, Santa Clara, Limousin oak

Gemello Zinfandel, Lot 71SC, Never oak (although strictly nonvintage by California law, most of this wine is from 1971 vintage; SC in the Lot number abbreviates Santa Clara)

These are very fine Zinfandels by any standard. But it is the remarkable study in contrast which makes these wines quite special. The wines complement each other so nicely that serving them together, particularly with a north Italian specialty such as Osso Bucco, is a very special experience in wine tasting and gastronomy.

The wine is from Gemello's Santa Clara vineyards on the slopes which rise up from the west side of the valley above Cupertino and Mountain View. These are among the most ideally situated vineyards in California. This is truly "mountain grown" Zinfandel with excellent sugar/acid balance.

It is the Gemello style to pick the grapes a bit earlier to retain zesty acidity rather than to pick later to achieve soft fruitiness and a degree or two more alcohol. They are made with a very definite European frame of reference in mind. As a result, they are more likely to appeal to a palate which has been educated on European wine. The higher acidity gives its own emphasis to the fruit extract. There are no strong reminiscences of other fruits. They are very "grapey" wines, having what the French call excellent "vinosity".

In appearance, the Zinfandel-Limousin looks something like a Burgundy; a cleaner, brighter ruby than the Zinfandel-Nevers which is slightly darker with a tinge of purple.

The Zinfandel-Limousin is generally a lighter, more subtle wine, leaning toward the style of Burgundy. There is the distinct trace of "vanilla" on the nose, characteristic of Limousin oak. The Zinfandel-Nevers is distinctly reminiscent of Bordeaux, but with a strong obeisance to the style of Chianti Classico; rather like an Italian winemaker's dream of some ideal Claret! This Zinfandel-Nevers has a fuller, more distinct grape-and-oak nose.

On the palate, the Zinfandel-Limousin is more advanced, more ready than the Zinfandel-Nevers which is still a bit backward with distinctly more wood tannin. The Zinfandel-Limousin is finely textured while the Zinfandel-Nevers has considerably greater depth of fruit; generally a more robust, chewy wine. Both are absolutely first-rate Zinfandels.

Another superb Zinfandel-Nevers was made at Chateau Montelena (Napa) in 1973. This wine is just beginning to develop its extraordinary potential.

All of these Zinfandels, in spite of the use of French oak, show a distinctly California style of winemaking. The overall philosophy is to let the fruit predominate as much as possible; other factors are valued for the way that they contribute toward that end. The wines make admirably straightforward statements. This contrasts with French style which prizes greater subtlety of statement, finesse and breed. It is fascinating, then, to see what a French winemaker can do with the Zinfandel grape. Bernard Portet, winemaker at Clos du Val (Napa), is a member of a French family which has been involved in the wine business for generations. Portet also has a degree in viticulture and enology from the University of Montpelier. His first Zinfandel opens up a whole new slant on the grape.

Clos du Val Zinfandel, 1972, Napa

tasted at three and one half years old

The wine has a marvelous dark ruby glow; tears form as the wine slides down the side of the glass, indicating an abundance of glycerol.

Contrasted with *any* fruity California Zinfandel, the wine, on the nose, has a great deal of French oak but, curiously, the oak does not *contrast* with the fruit. The bouquet impresses in the manner of a big, fleshy Pomerol. (Lovers of French Pomerol will enjoy this wine!) The nose is scented, balanced and very complex. The fruit is muted, subtle, at the service of the overall complexity. Many of the values of Zinfandel are there in complex balance: the raspberry character, the slight peppery quality, the vaguely Port-like character (the wine has a nice sweet aroma) but none of these stand out awkwardly. It seems a contradiction of terms to call this an elegant Zinfandel nose, but such is the case.

In the mouth, the wine is firm, dry and balanced. A great deal of attention has been given to acidity; there is a judicious trace of sweetness but not sufficient to give special emphasis to fruitiness, as is so often the case in the typical California style. And yet, Zinfandel is somehow not Zinfandel if it does not have a nice fruitiness in the mouth. This wine has an exceptional cherry-raspberry fruitiness set off by a very sturdy sugar/acid framework. Needless to say, the wine finishes beautifully. This wine could only have been made in California!

By no means are all Zinfandels made well enough to warrant laying down for further development. A great many California Zinfandels are just good drinking wines. Of these, there are some which are deliberately made in a very light manner, frivolous but enjoyable quaffing wine, inspired perhaps by young Beaujolais. The most exemplary Zinfandel made in this manner is the non-vintage Zinfandel of Nichelini Vineyards, east of the Napa Valley. This wine is far closer in style and taste to French Beaujolais than virtually any of the "Gamay Beaujolais" made in California, so many of which are utterly vapid wines. If your Nichelini Zinfandel has a ragged edge or two, give it another few months in your cellar and by that time you will be hard-pressed to distinguish it from a nice frisky Beaujolais.

In 1973, some light Zinfandels were made in exactly the same manner as French "Beaujolais Nouveau" using the *carbonic maceration* technique. This technique is not a recent development. Actually, it is based on a very old winemaking method, in which the grapes are placed in an open vat and are partially crushed by stamping feet. A great many whole berries remain in the fermenting must. The juice and partially crushed skins ferment in the usual manner but there is also a partial fermentation which takes place *within each of the whole berries.* When the fermentation is well advanced, free run and press juice are combined and the fermentation is completed in cask or closed container. There is remarkably little tannin extracted in this type of fermentation. The wine is ready to drink only a few months after the vintage.

In some of the more modern adaptations of this method, the first stage of fermentation (whole and partially crushed berries) takes place in an air-tight tank or cask under a cushion of carbon dioxide gas.

In vintage 1973, carbonic maceration Zinfandels were made at Grand Cru Vineyards (Sonoma County), Thomas Kruse (Gilroy, Santa Clara Valley), and at Monteviña in Amador County. The results are enormously encouraging. Although I enjoyed them all very much, my personal preference was for Gary Gott's:

Monteviña Zinfandel Nuevo, 1973, Amador County

tasted at nine months old

The wine is rather deeply pigmented, considerably darker than a Beaujolais. There is an immense fragrance of berries which fills the glass and perfumes the surrounding air. On the palate the wine is soft and delicious, a joy to drink. There is no rasping tannin and no disagreeably sharp acidity typical of very young wine.

At Dry Creek Vineyards (Sonoma County), Dave Stare has developed his own very interesting and successful variation on Zinfandel Nouveau. The grapes are stemmed and crushed as in normal winemaking procedure, but the must is cool-fermented in a temperature controlled stainless steel vat. In this method a great deal of fruit acid and fresh fruit aroma is retained. The wine is attractive when it is very young, but has somewhat more staying power than carbonic maceration wines.

For many years it was the practice in the central valley to leave a portion of Zinfandel on the vine to develop a few extra degrees of sugar. A sweet, Port type wine was made from these grapes by arresting the fermentation with several percentage points of sugar remaining. This was done by adding sufficient distilled grape wine spirits to bring the alcohol up to 19%–20%.

It was not until 1968 that the first experiments in late-harvest and White Zinfandel were made in the north coast vineyards. Ridge Vineyards, always a great pioneer in developing the possibilities of premium wines in California, was one of the first to experiment with the higher possibilities of late-harvest Zinfandel. A small lot of what Ridge called "Zinfandel Essence" was made from a special November picking of Zinfandel grapes which had developed botrytis mold and an unprecedented 35° sugar. This Zinfandel was decidedly sweet, strictly a dessert wine.

An even more celebrated late-harvest Zinfandel was made in the same year, during Bob Travers' first year at Mayacamas Vineyards. Although the sugar rose to 29°, Bob was able to ferment the wine to dryness, giving 17% alcohol. This was quite unprecedented because it was assumed that yeasts could not survive all that alcohol. The small quantity which came onto the market was snapped up so fast that relatively few (myself not included) got to taste this legendary wine. Fortunately we have a second-hand pleasure in reading Harry Waugh's fine report of the wine in the book, *Diary of a Winetaster*.

Leo Trentadue's first year at his newly purchased winery in the Alexander Valley was 1969; and he had the same experience as Bob Travers with late-harvest red grapes with botrytis. In this case the compostion of the grapes was somewhat different. It had long been the custom of Italian winemakers in California to plant vineyards of mixed varieties, and to harvest and vinify the grapes together. This particular section of the Trentadue Estate was planted to Zinfandel (for berry brightness and character), Petite Sirah (for deep color and spicy-peppery varietal interest) and Carignane (a relatively neutral, prolific variety to increase yield). As Leo relates in the notes on the back of the bottle: "During the 1969 vintage we by-passed a particular section of vines to let them develop more sugar. An early rain came, so we assumed the section was gone. Rain then typically means bunch-rot and hopeless spoilage. Late in the fall we discovered the 'rot' wasn't the usual one, but the rarely occuring botrytis cinerea; it accentuates sugar by leeching moisture and not spoiling. The rain had been just soft enough and the temperature had remained warm. We picked. Sugar was an unbelievable 34° brix. We had a collector's item."

Trentadue "Chateau 32", Late-Harvest Burgundy, 1969, Alexander Valley (17.5% alcohol)

tasted at five years old

Very deep, dark ruby, slightly tawny at the edge of the glass. The wine rolls down the side of the glass in sheets which taper into large "tears". It looks very much like a fine Ruby Port. Complex, overwhelming nose. There is something in the complex which reminds one of the aroma of prunes and dried apricots which have steeped in brandy, or perhaps something reminiscent of the aroma of nicely aged mincemeat. There is a background scent of herbs and spices and the pungent aroma of American oak. A tremendous, alcoholic nose. Captivating, but the olfactory organisms quickly become anaesthetized with all that alcohol! It is necessary to come up occasionally for a rest!

On the palate, huge and mouthfilling with a luxurious velvety texture. Heaps of fruit. The wine is thick with layer upon layer of flavor. The wine was neither fined nor filtered and, although there was considerable sediment, one senses that there was nothing fine taken away or sterilized out of this wine. The wine is really quite different from Port. It is medium-dry, with lots of residual sugar balancing a surprisingly crisp and refreshing acidity. There is an interesting and complementary bitter edge on the finish.

I could hardly think of a finer wine to serve with an array of *very* ripe, *very* aromatic French cheeses, among them might be a soft-ripening double crème; a pungent, well advanced goat cheese; and a good, strong Roquefort; served with San Francisco sour dough bread.

I single out this wine because it was available at the winery for several months at a very reasonable price. Eventually the wine was "discovered" and there was a terrific run on the remaining stock. Naturally, Leo raised the price and put a limit on purchases. The moral is that with a little patient digging around some of the less highly publicized wineries, one can turn up some really outstanding wine at very reasonable prices.

Dr. David Bruce has become something of a master in the art of making late-harvest Zinfandel. He uses grapes from the Hecker Pass district near Gilroy in the lower Santa Clara Valley. There is generally no botrytis, but there are a great many raisins among the grapes and the must reaches a very high brix reading.

My own experience has been with the 1971 vintage which includes three different late-harvest Zinfandels: one dry version at 15% alcohol and two different versions at 17.5% alcohol, one very dry and the other semi-dry.

David Bruce Late-Harvest Zinfandel, 1971, Santa Clara Valley
(17.5% alcohol, semi-dry)

tasted at three and one half years old

Brilliantly clear, lustrous garnet. Exciting alcoholic nose with a very clean, uncomplicated aroma of raisined Zinfandel. There is a lot of White American oak which creates a very taut structural balance against all the alcohol and the Zinfandel aroma. Very clean and silky on the palate with a slightly bitter finish which is perfectly integrated into the wine.

A beautifully crafted wine which should improve and develop complexity for many years. As it is now, this wine would be marvelous to serve all by itself to enhance spirited and racy conversation among very special friends.

The warm, energetic, quickwitted personality of Dr. Bruce seems to be reflected in this wine.

Although it seems that White Zinfandel was fairly common in the early days of California winemaking, it was not until the mid-sixties that Ridge Vineyards and David Bruce produced White Zinfandels. The practice of making a white wine from red grapes is not entirely novel. Most of French champagne is made from red wine grapes, especially Pinot Noir.

White Zinfandels are distinctly different wines. There is a unique fullness of aroma and flavor which sets them apart and gives them a justifiable place in the cellar.

One of the more interesting White Zinfandels was made at Sutter Home.

Sutter Home "Oeil de Perdrix", White Zinfandel, 1972, Amador County

tasted at two years old

There is a lovely peach hue to this wine. On the nose, a delicate aroma, only vaguely reminiscent of red Zinfandel. Rather than raspberries, one is reminded of ripe figs. Surprisingly deep flavored on the palate, quite dry, moderate acidity, with a very distinct and attractive bitterness on the finish. Because of this bitter edge, I would be inclined to place the wine as an aperitif, rather than as a wine to accompany food. The wine is similar in effect to that refreshing apertitif of Burgundy known as "Kir"—very dry, young white wine (usually Aligoté) to which is added a few drops of Dijon Crème de Cassis (black currant liquer). In the case of the White Zinfandel, the slightly bitter finish sets it apart, making it especially appetite provoking.

Perhaps the finest White Zinfandel I have tasted was the 1973 White Zinfandel of Monteviña (Amador County). The production was so small that relatively few people had the opportunity to taste this —hopefully there will be a great deal more of this splendid wine in the future.

Monteviña White Zinfandel, 1973, Amador County

tasted at one and one quarter years old

There is a faint peach (or perhaps salmon?) hue to the wine—just lovely to look at. In a blind tasting (in this case it would have to be a blindfold tasting!) one would be tempted to say Chardonnay on the nose, so big and full is the aroma of this wine. There is just the slightest hint of the berry character of red Zinfandel. On the palate, the wine compares to a Chardonnay as a Blanc de Noir Champagne (made from Pinot Noir grapes) compares to a Blanc de Blancs Champagne (made from Chardonnay and/or Pinot Blanc grapes). Very meaty and full for being a "white" wine, and yet not in the least bit heavy. It has all the freshness and buoyancy of a white wine, but somewhat greater body and depth of flavor; exceptional acidity and a remarkably good finish. A completely appetizing wine.

Salmon has always been a difficult fish to match with wine. The slightly oily, very flavorsome meat of the salmon wants something just a bit fuller than most white wines. I cannot imagine a more perfect wine for grilled fresh salmon than this Monteviña White Zinfandel!

California Chardonnay

and Pinot Blanc

Ten

In the late 1950's, a California Chardonnay appeared on the market under the Hanzell Vineyard label at the unprecedented price of $6.00 per bottle. It took some non-believers a while to stop grumbling and pay the price, for the word was out that this was no ordinary California white wine. It was a rich, melon-fruity wine with a curious nutty character which reminded everyone of fine White Burgundy. No one thought that such a wine could be made in California.

The wine was the culmination of a secret ambition of J. D. Zellerbach to make wine in California which would be equal in quality to the great French Burgundies. After his retirement in 1948 as American Ambassador to Italy, Zellerbach, in association with winemaker Brad Webb, had a vineyard of Chardonnay and Pinot Noir planted out on the westward slope of the Mayacamas Range, overlooking the town of Sonoma. In building the winery, they settled for nothing less than the best equipment, the most sophisticated winery design and the finest French oak cooperage. In California, this was probably the first full realization of the crucial importance of the aging container in the making of premium wines. Eventually, California wine lovers became aware that the "nutty" characteristic of Hanzell Chardonnay and some French White Burgundy was actually a flavor derived from oak.

The use of the finest French oak cooperage was not the only innovation at Hanzell. It was Brad Webb, at Hanzell, who developed the use of temperature controlled stainless steel fermentation tanks for the first time in California.

Perhaps no other white wine made in California has had such a great influence. The first Hanzell wines coincided with the start of the imported wine boom in this country. There was a great deal of interest in French White Burgundy, most of which is made from Chardonnay. Zellerbach and Webb proved, beyond a shadow of a doubt, that a great Chardonnay could be made in California. The fine Chardonnays of Fred McCrea at Stony Hill and of the Taylors at Mayacamas were supporting evidence. On the strength of these early successes, a great many new Chardonnay vineyards were planted which came into production in the late 1960's. Both 1969 and 1970 were exceptional years for Chardonnay and several fine wines were made. We are finally in a position to assess some of the wide ranging possibilities of Chardonnay in California.

It has been discovered that although region I (comparable to the Côte de Beaune in France) seemed to be the most appropriate for Chardonnay by virtue of high acid retention, Chardonnay grown in region II and even in the coolest end of region III could produce wines of immense fruit even though the acidity was relatively low. A very cool, patient fermentation would retain a great deal of fruitiness in addition to a sufficient amount of fruit acid. Provided that the wine did not spend too much time in oak and was drunk reasonably early while it was still young and fresh; a big, luscious Chardonnay could be made in a climate which was considerably warmer than Burgundy. There is a general feeling that it is not as crucial to quality to grow Chardonnay on hillside terrain. Whereas the best Johannisberg Riesling seems to come from hillside vineyards; this is not necessarily the case with Chardonnay.

Because of the wider range of climatic differences in California, the general stylistic range of California Chardonnay is broader and more varied than French Chardonnay. Differences among French Chardonnays seem to stem more from soil differences along the Côte d'Or, in Chablis, and farther south in the Côte Mâconnais and Côte Chalonaise. There are incredibly varied flavor nuances. The differences are subtle and fascinating. In California the emphasis is on the fruit, balanced by flavors derived from cooperage—differences seem to be based on the relative richness of fruit and the way in which fruit and oak flavors complement each other on the palate.

California Chardonnay does not seem to have the longevity of French

White Burgundy. Although it is ready much sooner, there is a tendency in California Chardonnay to reach its peak quite beautifully and then start to fade within a year. The difference in acidity between the French and California versions has a great deal to do with this. Most French Chardonnay is hard and acidic when it is young, requiring several years of softening before it reaches its peak. But unlike California Chardonnay it is also two years or more before it starts its gradual decline. A French Chardonnay which has reached its peak at eight years old is not altogether uncommon; a California Chardonnay which would reach that age in its best condition would be unusual. Ironically, several of the very top California Chardonnays seem to be exceptions to this rule. Of these, certainly the 1970 Sterling Vineyards Chardonnay (Napa) seems to get better and better every year and might well become one of the most extraordinary California Chardonnays ever made.

There might be an additional reason for these differences in longevity. The widely held belief in California that free run juice gives the best white wine may have something to do with the case. A Burgundian would laugh at this assumption. In France it is the belief that the juice derived from the first light pressing often provides the greatest depth of character. The traces of tannin derived from the press wine help the longevity of the wine, but they also make the wine hard in the early years. In the case of French White Burgundy, these residual tannins fade away at about the same rate as the acidity comes into balance. In California there is a danger that the lower acidity might fade well before the coarseness of the press wine recedes. Consequently, many California winemakers are reluctant to use press wine in premium Chardonnay. An exception would be the Chardonnay of Charles Krug which contains more press wine than most other Chardonnays in California. The 1969 vintage Krug Pinot Chardonnay, for example, suddenly bloomed into an extraordinary wine along about its fourth or fifth year.

Of those Chardonnays which use French oak cooperage, there is a broad stylistic range. At one end of the spectrum, the wines are lovely, delicate but intensely flavored. Hanzell and Chappellet Chardonnays and the older Souverain Chardonnays of Lee Stewart are made in this style. Joe Heitz has made some very soft, delicate and subtly shaded Chardonnays. At the opposite end of the spectrum, there are huge, full-bodied Chardonnays, rich in flavors derived from Limousin oak. Dr. David Bruce has made an exceptional series of Chardonnays in this style. And there are a great many fine Chardonnays in the middle of these stylistic extremes —the Chardonnays of Spring Mountain Vineyards (especially the 1971 and 1972 vintages), Robert Mondavi, and Mayacamas are in this range.

One of the finest of the more subtle California Chardonnays was this:

Hanzell Vineyards Chardonnay, 1970, Sonoma

tasted at four years old

Straw yellow with a touch of gold. On the nose, there is a flinty, Chardonnay aroma and perfectly integrated oak, reminiscent of Chablis Grand Cru in an exceptional year. This is phenomenally good wine! The wine is very dry and elegant in the mouth with exceptional acidity. But there is a shy smile of delicate fruit which places this wine somewhere beyond French Chablis. The wine is so appetizing that it sets one to thinking immediately of food, more specifically of superb fish. This wine has been an elegant accompaniment to an impeccably fresh, poached, Monterey Rock Cod served with a beurre blanc. It would also be admirable with Pacific Rex Sole, sauté Meuniere.

As the wine opens up, the flinty aroma develops into a delicate aroma which is faintly reminiscent of tea. The wine becomes a bit fuller in the mouth, with the subtlest hint of slightly raisined Chardonnay grapes. Finally, way back on the palate, there is a *goût de terrior* which places the wine in California. The finest French Limousin oak is used with a great deal of restraint.

Lee Stewart's 1969 Souverain Chardonnay was another of those California Chardonnays which inspired memories of superb Grand Cru Chablis. Similar to the 1970 Hanzell but with perhaps less acidity and a touch more residual sugar, this was a wine for Rex or Dover sole sauced with a velouté enriched with cream and butter or perhaps fish quenelles in a Nantua type sauce. This wine reached its peak at about three years old and then declined sooner than one would have hoped.

Certainly one of the most legendary California wines was the superb 1969 Spring Mountain Chardonnay. This wine was actually a cooperative venture of Mike Robbins, owner of Spring Mountain Vineyards, and Joe Heitz. Mike's own Chardonnay vineyards were several years away from full production so that, in order to build up the reputation of Spring Mountain wines, Mike contracted with other growers and wineries to make wines in association with him. In 1969 the Chardonnay was made in conjunction with Joe Heitz. Actually, it was a skillful blending of the Heitz regular Chardonnay (from vineyards at the foot of Mount Veeder) with the Chardonnay from Zinfandel Associates vineyard. My own notes on the two Heitz Chardonnays concur with those of Harry Waugh who liked the bouquet of the regular wine and the taste of the Zinfandel Associates wine. It was the blending of these two in the Spring Mountain Chardonnay which made such a splendid wine.

Spring Mountain Pinot Chardonnay, 1969, Napa

tasted at three years old

This was a remarkably complex wine, and yet one with immediate and irresistible appeal. Pale yellow. Very full, absolutely lovely nose —lots of very ripe Chardonnay character, tremendous fruit reminding one of pears, melon and yellow Santa Rosa plums. There are muted aromas derived from French oak and an intriguing Napa *goût de terroir*.

On the palate, there are flavors of superbly ripe fruit; the oak makes one think briefly of Meursault but, again, the wine is beyond French White Burgundy. It is the lack of crisp acidity which sets it apart from French Chardonnay. Rather, its youthful freshness keeps this big wine balanced and alive on the palate. This is a luscious, elegant, almost creamy textured wine in the mouth.

Curiously, the wine proved to be just a shade too big for richly sauced fresh lobster meat served in butter puff-pastry shells. It found an excellent match against sweetbreads in a rich cream sauce and was even more splendid against a very rich, unctuous slice of truffled *foie gras*.

But like the Souverain Chardonnay, it was showing lots of gray hairs well before its fourth year.

Among the medium weight wines which are reminiscent of French White Burgundy, there is a fine wine made, not from Chardonnay, but from Pinot Blanc grapes at Chalone Vineyards in Monterey County.

Pinot Blanc is not related to Chardonnay. Actually it is a clone of Pinot Noir. There is a great deal of confusion on this point because the French use the name "Pinot Blanc" as an alternate designation for Chardonnay. They reserve the name "Pinot Blanc Vrais" for the (true) Pinot Blanc which is grown in California.

Most of the Pinot Blancs from Chalone have had a heavy overlay of Limousin oak when they are first released. But the acidity is quite sufficient to sustain the wine while the raw oak flavors tone down and become integrated into the wine. These wines take at least two and a half years to even approach maturity and they generally manage to develop nicely past their fourth year.

Pinot Blanc has considerably less of the big, mouth-filling flavors of Chardonnay. The shading of flavors on the palate is rich and complex but, as Bob Thompson put it, "more agreeably subtle than Chardonnay at its fullest."

Chalone Vineyards is situated some 2000 feet above sea level, high above the town of Soledad in the Salinas Valley. This is a cool region I vineyard with optimum access to cooling air from Monterey Bay. This river of air is carried along the Salinas Valley air corridor and up the eastern slope of the valley. The soil is unusual for California, being quite similar to the soil complex along the Côte d'Or: rough textured topsoil with some red clay and a substructure of limestone-based soils. Limestone soil, so typical of the Côte d'Or, is unusual in California.

Chalone Vineyards Pinot Blanc, 1969, Monterey County

tasted at three years old

A sparkling clear and lively pale yellow. Big flowery-fruity bouquet, very fresh and clean, with a nice hint of Limousin oak and a curious smoky-flinty aroma which one tries in vain to place somewhere between Chablis and Pouilly Fumé. Curiously, this wine also bears a distinct and uncanny resemblance to Chassagne-Montrachet of a good vintage.

On the palate, very dry, rich and perfectly balanced. There is a slight hint of sweetness. One has the feeling that the wine was made from grapes which were picked at the exact moment of perfect ripeness. Unlike Chardonnay, which is very full and insistent on the palate, the wine is totally refreshing, clean and thirst-quenching. Reminiscent of fresh, cool, mountain spring water. This wine made an impressive showing against a *vol au vent* filled with *fruits de mer* in a rich lobster sauce.

The 1971 Chalone Pinot Blanc is a much bigger, full-bodied wine, very different in style from the 1969. The wine is packed with the flavors of luscious, very ripe fruit; it is slightly heady with alcohol and there is a heavy overlay of Limousin Oak. But like the 1970 Sterling Chardonnay, this wine seems to be getting better and better every time I taste it. The fruit and oak are gradually marrying together and the wine is becoming very complex. This Chalone Pinot Blanc seems to be holding on to its acidity very nicely and will possibly reach its peak in its sixth year.

The Chardonnays of Dr. David Bruce and Mt. Eden Vineyards in Santa Clara are very much in the same style, but with far more intensity of fruit (characteristic of Chardonnay) and almost overwhelming Limousin oak character. All of these wines need at least five years before one can begin to taste them properly. In the case of Chalone, Dr. David Bruce and Mt. Eden, the vineyards are so high up in the hills that they can maintain good acidity and still develop the extra sugar which makes them such big wines. All of these wines are very controversial, particularly in their younger years. I can recall a Chardonnay tasting in which a David Bruce Chardonnay received five first place votes and four last place votes while the only remaining taster placed it in the middle of a range of eight Chardonnays! Frankly, we have not had enough of these huge Limousin oak Chardonnays develop to their full potential to be able to make any sure judgements. Perhaps the most extraordinary of these big Chardonnays was this:

David Bruce Late Harvest Chardonnay, 1973, Santa Clara

tasted at two and one half years old

According to the back label, the grapes were harvested in mid-October from Dr. Bruce's own vineyard 2,000 feet above the Pacific Ocean in the Santa Cruz Mountains. The grapes were then fermented on the skins for three weeks at 60°–65° F. The wine underwent little, if any, filtering or fining.

It was necessary to rest the wine upright for two weeks and then decant very carefully. Even then, the deep Chardonnay yellow was a bit clouded with suspended particles. (If anyone takes offense at this lack of perfect clarity, I will be very happy to take your glass!)

One's nose is greeted at first with a powerful, pungently medicinal aroma which gives way, as one gets into the wine, to incredibly rich Chardonnay fruit with Limousin oak character in abundance. One is reminded of drippingly sweet, tree-ripened nectarines, of bananas in perfect ripeness; marvelously mellow, slightly heady (15.5% alcohol). There is a touch of butter-caramel as the wine blooms in the glass.

On the palate, huge body, wonderfully tangy, mouthfilling; there are reminiscences of apricots and tangerines. All that fruit and oak is kept alive by exceptionally good acidity; medium dry with a very distinct sweet edge to it. This wine is just beginning its glorious career.

The wine was superb, by itself, following a dessert of bananas which had been sautéed in butter, glazed toward the end with a fine, unprocessed beekeeper's honey and then flamed with a fruity California brandy.

The Freemark Abbey Chardonnays are somewhat of a departure from the Limousin oak Chardonnays and Pinot Blancs.

Freemark Abbey Pinot Chardonnay, 1970, Napa

tasted at four years old

This is a big fat Chardonnay, typical Freemark Abbey yellow with a touch of gold. Rich, fruity Chardonnay nose, accented quite beautifully with Nevers rather than Limousin oak. This Chardonnay/oak fills the mouth with intense flavors. There is a slightly higher than normal alcoholic weight to the wine (13.4% alcohol). The reasonably good acidity is softened and muted by the higher alcohol, but the flavor intensity and body (the result of careful viticulture and very ripe grapes) is so big that one can be quite satisfied with the lower acidity.

Nevers oak is the oak of Red Bordeaux. In this Chardonnay, the oak hangs in the mouth so distinctly (much less subtly than Limousin) that one can almost imagine a light red wine in the place of the white wine. The fruit is so rich, though, that all the fruit balances the oak very appropriately.

This very rich wine needs the right food context: buttery crepes rolled around thin slices of ham and chopped spinach, napped with a very positive mournay sauce; a fine roast loin of pork; or roast duckling garnished with poached white figs.

A very rich, high alcohol Chardonnay was made at Burgess Cellars (Napa) in 1973. This wine is made from Carneros (region I) grapes and is considerably higher in acid than the Freemark Abbey Chardonnay. Rather awkward at the moment, there are indications that this wine might well become an extraordinary Chardonnay in two or three years.

The 1971 and 1972 Pinot Chardonnays of Mike Robbins' Spring Mountain Vineyards are quite possibly the most classic of all the Napa Chardonnays. Several other Napa Chardonnays are similar in style to these wines but Spring Mountain seems to set the pace and the high standards.

The grapes are crushed and fermented at another winery and then cellared and bottled at Spring Mountain. These wines attest to the crucial importance of proper cellaring in the winemaking process. Wine is incredibly sensitive both to its aging container and the cellar environment in which it develops. Wine responds very positively to the special care and attention to detail which an astute winemaker lavishes on the young wines. Lee Stewart was one of the first and most influential winemakers in California to espouse and emphasize this philosophy of meticulous care of the wines in the cellar and the major difference it makes in the quality of the wine.

Spring Mountain Pinot Chardonnay, 1971, Napa

tasted at two and one half years old

Spring Mountain Pinot Chardonnay, 1972, Napa

tasted at two and one half years old

There is plenty of Limousin oak in these wines but the fruit definitely has the upper hand. These Chardonnays are not as soft as the Chardonnays of Heitz or Freemark Abbey; nor are they strongly reminiscent of French White Burgundy. These wines are unmistakably and inimitably Californian.

While the 1971 was pale yellow, slightly steely, more austere, the 1972 was a rich yellow with a touch of gold and was richer in fruit. There is a strong backbone which runs through the fruit and the oak of both these wines. Big, authoritative, beautifully balanced, these wines represent the culmination of the specifically Napa style of Chardonnay.

These are very versatile wines but they are of such quality that they demand elegant foods. They are perhaps at their best served with foods which have a distinctly California bias: artichoke bottoms or halves of avocado stuffed with the meat of tiny bay shrimp bound in a tomato flavored mayonnaise, perhaps given a bright yellow "mimosa" garnish; cracked dungeness crab which has been lightly marinated in olive oil, white wine vinegar, chopped fresh basil and a hint of garlic; chilled fresh Monterey Bay prawns served with a creamy tomato mousse; or perhaps breast of chicken Veronique.

There are other California Chardonnays which are distinctly different and individual in style. No wine lover in his right mind can come to California Chardonnay with a preconceived notion of what a Chardonnay should be like! Rather than trying to force these wines into a preconceived scale of taste values and onto a rating chart, one should appreciate and enjoy the sheer variety of style in California Chardonnay. Imaginative gourmets should exult in this bountiful variety and accept the challenge which these fine wines present.

One of the finer, more individual Chardonnays was this:

Charles Krug Pinot Chardonnay, 1969, Napa

tasted at five years old

This wine started out in a rather matter-of-fact manner. The price was reasonable and the wine was agreeable enough to drink with just about any food which needed a white wine with basically good acidity.

By its fifth year, this wine had opened up and bloomed into a very special, quite extraordinary wine. Somewhat deeper yellow than most Chardonnays; a marvelously full bouquet, lots of fruit, a hint of succulent vine-ripened melon, and a distinctly different oak aroma. Krug used Yugoslav oak cooperage for this wine, and the effect is quite distinct and individual.

A complex, luscious wine on the palate, still quite lively with acidity. In terms of quality, it is right up there with fine French Chardonnay. The wine has the "stuffing" of White Burgundy and yet the wine is so individual that the comparison seems almost odious. The wine was especially fine with chicken, small white onions and mushrooms in a buttery sauce suprème.

Beaulieu Pinot Chardonnay, 1970, Napa/Carneros

tasted at four years old

This was another very unusual, individual, un-classic, un-French Chardonnay of extraordinary quality. Very pale yellow, there seems to be relatively little oak on the nose; rather, an intense "herb garden" aroma. Full and elegant in the mouth with excellent acidity. This wine poses one of the most interesting gastronomic puzzles: so fine and individual a wine wants a very special food context. One rather successful match was made with a classic Poulet Rôti à l'Estragon: a plump chicken is stuffed with fresh tarragon leaves, roasted, carved and served with a few spoonfuls of rich chicken half-glaze. The wine was also a fine accompaniment to a plate of freshly made green noodles (spinach and watercress), served with Bolognese sauce and freshly grated Romano cheese.

Wente Brothers Pinot Chardonnay, 1972, Livermore Valley, Estate Bottled

tasted at two and one half years old

This is another very un-French, very individual Chardonnay of exceptional quality. The wine is a major departure in that it is made and aged in containers other than wood. But there are additional reasons why this wine is so markedly different from any other Chardonnay made in California.

The Livermore Valley has a very individual climate and soil which sets it apart and puts its stamps on the wines. In summer, the valley is a shade warmer than Napa. The air is warm (perhaps 90°) and the sun is bright and intense. But there are ameliorating breezes which create an ambiance of pleasant vigor rather than soporific mid-summer heat. The soil is very porous and gravelly; the dust of the earth gets into the nostrils—there is an unmistakable aroma of the earth which pervades the atmosphere.

This Wente Chardonnay is quite distinctly yellow with a tint of the grassy gold of California hills in summer. There is an aroma of lovely ripe fruit but there is also an intriguing aroma of earth which one remembers from past summers in the valley. There is no intrusive oak, just the interplay of fruit and the aroma of the land on which it was grown.

How distinctly different on the palate! There is a richness of flavor and body, typical of Chardonnay, and a fullness of ripe fruit which fills the mouth. The wine is refreshingly dry with a gentle acidity. A distinct taste of the earth plays against the fruit. There is a simplicity of statement and yet a complexity and balance of aromas and flavors as one gets into the wine. This Chardonnay is very classic in its unencumbered reflection of fruit and earth.

This is not a wine for seafood or poultry—the softness of acidity emphasizes the fruit too distinctly. This was a lovely wine served with prosciutto and melon—the pungency of the ham set off the *goût de terroir* of the wine while the melon and the ripe Chardonnay flavors complimented each other very nicely. As an entree wine, it was superb against Saltimbocca Romana. And what an exceptional value for money is this wine!

California Johannisberg Riesling

Eleven

There are two basic approaches to making a Johannisberg Riesling. The first is to make a very basic white wine without any elaborate cellar treatment and put it in large (preferably German) oak barrels of 100 gallons or more for anywhere from six months to two years. Most of the older California and German Rieslings were made in this manner. The method still survives in some California wineries and in some of the more southerly German wine districts. They are rich, perhaps heavy wines (they have been described as Wagnerian), medium dry and soft, with big earthy and woody flavors. These are good wines for accompanying, say, duckling or rabbit.

The second approach is relatively new in Germany, the result of both a very sophisticated wine technology and some extraordinary vineyard conditions. The objective of this method is to produce Riesling which on the one hand is very crisp and delicate and on the other has great intensity of flavor and finesse. Very little, if any oak is used in this method. The wine is intended to be very fresh and very clean. To this end, the Germans developed temperature controlled fermentation and special centrifuges to render the wine clean and brilliant without the need for excessive filtering. Most of the great Rieslings of the Rheingau and the Moselle regions are made in this manner.

The Rheingau and Moselle regions are the most northerly viticultural districts which produce great wines. The vineyards are perched on the slopes which rise rather precipitously from the rivers. The best of these vineyards are banked so that they receive the full daylight sun virtually at right angles (i.e., where the rivers flow east to west and the vineyards are on the northern bank). There is excellent air circulation and the proximity to water tempers the air so that there are no radical swings in temperature. These are basically what a Californian would call "mountain" growing conditions. Although these far northern vineyards have optimum access to sunlight when it occurs, the summers can be very cloudy and the grapes might not ripen at all. But when proper ripening does occur, there are extraordinary balances created between high sugar and high acid. This framework is so sturdy that it can carry the delicately flavored wines to dizzying heights. These wines can be true "bottled poetry", wines perhaps better suited for meditation or intimate conversation rather than the conviviality of the table. Rheingau Riesling, though, has a remarkable affinity to lobster and I believe it was Ken Kew and Karl Petrowsky who first recommended serving Rheingau Rieslings with Chinese cuisine.

Some growers will gamble and leave the grapes on the vine an extra two to four weeks to develop extra sugar. The mists which rise from the river at night, or gentle rains, will dampen the grape clusters. As the autumn sun warms the dampened grapes, the condition known as "noble mold" (botrytis cinerea) will sometimes occur. Water in the grape juices will evaporate through the skins and the film of mold, acidity is left intact, and the sugars and flavor extracts become more concentrated. Whether or not the mold occurs, the grapes go into the making of the famous "late-picked" or *"spaetlese"* wines. Often, a separate picking of particularly ripe or moldy clusters is made—perhaps one or two clusters from the several on the vine. This is for the more costly "special picking" or *"auslese"* wines. Finally, a very special late picking of *individual berries* is made: these are for the *"beerenauslese"* wines ("special harvest of berries") and *"trockenbeeren-auslese"* ("special harvest of rasined berries"). These wines are progressively more and more intense in the flavors of honey, wild-flowers and luscious, sweet fruit. One bottle of *trockenbeerenauslese* is the equivalent of at least a dozen bottles of wine made with an equal number of normally ripened grapes. Understandably, the bottles are priced like full cases of wine.

Grape clusters which are attacked with botrytis mold are particularly ugly looking. During the 1972 grape harvest in California, a Napa Valley grower showed up at a prestigious winery with a load of Johannisberg Riesling grapes which had been attacked by botrytis. The grower was told something like, "Don't insult our intelligence by trying to sell us rotten grapes!" Fortunately, a well known winemaker happened to be on the scene and told the grower to bring the "rotten" grapes over to his place —that he would take them off his hands. One of the very finest California Rieslings was made from those grapes!

This story illustrates the extremes of imaginative thinking and hidebound thinking which are typical of the California wine scene. Unfortunately, Johannisberg Riesling has largely been treated just like any other grape variety; but if ever there was a grape variety which demands very individual treatment, it is the Riesling.

Contrary to common belief, botrytis mold is not rare in California. There is often at least one light rain by early October. Vineyards which are close enough to the bay or the ocean to be affected by damp sea mists and fog will also develop botrytis mold.

As one would expect, Dave Bennion at Ridge was the first to experiment with late harvest Riesling grapes affected with botrytis. In 1966, small lots of *beerenauslese* and *trockenbeerenauslese* were made from botrytised Johannisberg Riesling from Vine Hill Vineyard, Santa Cruz.

Up until the late 1960's most of the better California Johannisberg Rieslings were made in the "old" manner. The tendency was particularly strong to keep the wines in large oak casks or vats for at least a year or two "to develop character". They were soft, earthy wines which tended to be flabby. One of the major exceptions was an interesting series of Rieslings produced at Freemark Abbey beginning in the late 1960's. These were Rieslings made in the "old" manner, but the method was completely re-thought and adjusted to California conditions. Among the many fine Rieslings was:

Freemark Abbey Johannisberg Riesling, 1969, Lot 92, Conn Creek Vineyard, Napa Valley

tasted at three and one half years old

This was not a wine for those who prefer a very crisp, delicate Riesling. And yet how absurd it would be to let prejudices interfere with the enjoyment of this superb wine.

Riesling ripens quite early in California. One of the problems with late picking is that a significant amount of acid respires from the fruit in the warmth of the early autumn. By the time there is any rainfall which might induce botrytis, the acid is already somewhat low. This was the case with the Lot 92 Riesling. Botrytis finally did occur and sugar and extracts were greatly intensified.

The must had high sugar but relatively low acid. The wine was fermented dry, giving low residual sugar and high alcohol (13.7%). Under normal circumstances, this might not produce very satisfying results. But thanks to the restraint which Freemark maintains in refusing to over-crop their grapes, and aided by additional flavor intensification which results from botrytis, the fruit extract was so intense that it balanced out all that alcohol. A deep golden yellow, the wine was heady with the wild-flowers and honey aroma of Riesling with botrytis. The wine is very soft in the mouth, not zesty with acidity. But a very rich complex of extracts fills the mouth and lingers very insistently, in spite of the lack of a strong sugar/acid framework. The wine spent six months in large American oak tanks—just enough time for this big wine to absorb an interesting background of oak flavors.

Lee Stewart at Souverain was perhaps the first California winemaker to produce a truly delicate Riesling in the manner of the Moselle-Rheingau. His 1965 and 1968 Johannisberg Rieslings immediately gained him the reputation of being the foremost maker of Riesling in California. Subsequent vintages kept him very much in the running. A major portion of the grapes were from Jerry Draper's hillside vineyards on the west side of the Napa Valley. The approach was to pick the fruit with as much concern for acid as for sugar; that is, to pick at the exact point of ripeness at which the fruit would still have reasonably high acid and just enough sugar to make the minimum of alcohol and the appropriate amount of residual sugar to balance the acid. The fermentation was kept very cool and slow. Granted, the wines did not achieve the great sugar/acid contrasts of Moselle and Rheingau Rieslings, and they did not attain what Kathleen Bourke called the "crisp backbone" of German Rieslings; nevertheless, they were beautiful, delicate wines with a great deal of flowery Riesling character. The alcohol was kept fairly low so that it did not cover the acidity. The wine was not held in wood for long but was bottled and released early so that it could be drunk while it was still fresh and youthful.

During the early 1960's, new plantings of Riesling were made with particular attention to climatic conditions favorable to this variety. Important Riesling vineyards were planted in the Carneros district. Starting in 1969 some very promising Johannisberg Rieslings have been made at Z-D

Winery (Sonoma) from Carneros grapes. Fine Rieslings were made at Yverdon Vineyards, high in the Mayacamas Range. These latter were reminiscent of the Rieslings of Alsace.

The most important new planting of this period was done under the direction of Ernest Wente in Monterey County. Ernest was a noted vineyardist while Herman Wente was regarded by many as the greatest of the older generation of California winemakers. The Wente Brothers planted a vineyard of Johannisberg Riesling in the Arroyo Seco, deep in the Salinas Valley. This now famous vineyard and the great Rieslings it has given us could not have been a more appropriate gift to wine lovers from these two extraordinary pioneers of California premium wine.[1]

While technically in the Salinas Valley, Arroyo Seco is at the end of a canyon which connects with the Carmel Valley. There is also a small gap in the Coast Range which lets additional sea air into Arroyo Seco and, being

---

[1] There were a great many new plantings in the Salinas Valley during this period and many of these plantings were made with vines grown on their own rootstocks, as opposed to the normal procedure of grafting Vinifera vines onto resistant root stocks. This latter is an almost universal practice which prevents attack from a root louse known as Phylloxera. This is the same root louse which devastated European and California vineyards in the late 19th century. Phylloxera will attack the thinner, less hardy roots of Vinifera vines but is repelled by the thicker, more woody roots of native American (Labrusca) vines. Hence, the reason for grafting Vinifera vines onto specially developed, hardier root stocks. Sandy soil, however, is also inimical to the root louse. Since the soil complex of the Salinas Valley is based primarily on sand, Vinifera vines could be planted without grafting.

Although most of the plantings were made without grafting, Ernest Wente chose to plant his Arroyo Seco vineyard in the traditional manner. It is interesting to note one of the major reasons for his decision. In the more woody resistant root stocks, the flow of springtime sap is considerably slower than it is in the less hardy roots of Vinifera. The grafting of Vinifera onto these special root stocks serves as a natural deterrent to over-cropping and too quick and lush a growth of vines. His feeling was that it is very difficult to control over-cropping in Vinifera vines which are growing on their own roots. [See Wente, Ernest; *Winemaking in the Livermore Valley.* Berkeley: Univ. of Calif., Bancroft Library, 1971. Typescript.]

only twenty miles from the ocean, fog and mists are often carried along as far as the vineyard during the early autumn. This is a near perfect climatic complex for Johannisberg Riesling.

Wente Brothers Johannisberg Riesling Spaetlese, 1969, Arroyo Seco

tasted at three and one half years old

This was a memorable wine. Very pale yellow and bright. Shy but finally blooming on the nose—lovely Riesling aroma and a distinct hint of honey—accented by very muted earth flavors which made it unmistakably Californian. But the wine had the kind of balance of aromas which one finds only in superb German Riesling.

On the palate, semi-dry, a nice residual sweetness but not cloying; delicately honeyed Riesling with all those other complexities of flavor which botrytis seems to impart. Typically Californian, the emphasis is on the delicate but luscious fruit of the wine. Excellent acidity keeps the flavors alive all the way across the palate. Appetizing and utterly refreshing. Not so ethereal a Riesling as to make it difficult to serve with food. Matched with a cold Galantine of Duck as the opening course of an elaborate dinner, the rich Riesling flavors came up very elegantly. In another context, as a dessert wine served with a mélange of sliced fresh California fruit, with nothing but their own naturally sweet juices, the delicate honeyed sweetness of the wine came up beautifully.

A fine Riesling Spaetlese was made at Wente in 1972 and in 1973 both an Auslese and a Spaetlese were made. With additional years in the bottle the 1973 Auslese may well turn out to be the finest of the Wente Rieslings.

There were some early rains during the 1972 harvest in California, and the development of botrytis was not uncommon. The Napa Valley Riesling vineyard of Dick Steltzner was infected with botrytis and the grapes were purchased by Lyncrest Vineyards where they were made into a very fine Riesling Spaetlese. The vineyard is on an unusual outcropping of red clay soil, northeast of the city of Napa, on a slope which rises up to the mountain range on the east side of the valley. This is a region I vineyard which is particularly accessible to the damp fog and mists which come in from the bay.

Lyncrest Johannisberg Riesling Spaetlese, 1972, Napa

tasted at two years old

This is not a wine for every palate. It is an exceptionally delicate and subtle Riesling, especially by California standards, very much in the style of a Riesling Spaetlese of the Moselle. Winemaker John Henderson is a protégé of Lee Stewart and one can detect the influence of the master.

There is a faint greenish tinge to the delicate yellow—the wine looks like a Moselle. On the nose there is a delicate grape perfume of Riesling-with-botrytis set against a subtle background of American oak. On the palate one notices immediately the low alcoholic "weight" of the wine, so typical of German

Riesling but so rare in California. The wine is unusually mouth-filling for being so delicate. There is a slight bitter edge on the finish but this is more intriguing than objectionable and will probably fade.

Unfortunately, the price of this wine was rather out of line. Any number of fine Moselles of the great 1971 vintage could have been purchased for significantly less.

Three other late picked Rieslings were made in 1972, at Chateau Montelena and Beaulieu in Napa and at Sonoma Vineyards in the Russian River area of Sonoma County. The Beaulieu was made from grapes which had developed botrytis and was distinctly in the style of the Rheingau: delicate gold in color, full and pungent with Riesling aromas and flavors—a lovely wine.

In 1973 Sonoma Vineyards produced another Riesling Spaetlese (a nice Riesling-with-botrytis, superior to their 1972 version) and Chateau Montelena released a Riesling from the Alexander Valley which was labeled "Auslese". This was a very interesting late picked wine with a very distinct *goût de terroir* of the Alexander Valley, rather in the style of Free-mark Abbey. However, there was no botrytis character to this wine. Tasting this wine against any of the botrytis Rieslings I have mentioned will give some perspective on the botrytis character, which is literally a "noble rot"—there *is* a distinct "rotten" flavor characteristic to the wines; rotten, perhaps, but not in the least bit *spoiled* or *soured*, and therein lies the difference and the reason the French use the term *"pourriture noble"* or *"noble rot"*.

It should be realized that up to 1975, there were no laws which governed the use of such terms as "spaetlese" and "auslese" as they applied to California Rieslings. The United States government has since put a stop to the use of such designations. This is only fair to the consumer. In the future, winemakers should spell out on a back label the exact meaning of any alternate designations which they select for these wines. The back label on the 1972 Beaulieu Spaetlese could certainly serve as a model.

Two other exceptional Johannisberg Rieslings were made in 1973:

Beringer Johannisberg Riesling Auslese, 1973, Knights' Valley, Sonoma County

tasted at one and one half years old

This is the first wine from the new Beringer vineyard in Knights' Valley, an eastward extension of the Alexander Valley which narrows to a canyon which connects into the northern tip of the Sonoma Valley.

This is certainly one of the finest Rieslings ever made in California. Although the wine is Moselle-like in appearance, the nose is quite full and unlike either Moselle or Rheingau. In fact, attempts at comparison break down completely. This wine is on a very high level and stands completely on its own merits. This is a very individual wine.

Very pleasant, but complex nose. The contrasts are clearly drawn, nicely balanced and perfectly integrated. A classic, crisp Riesling aroma pervades; there is a soft, matte tone, a distinct

aroma of the earth which defines the wine as Californian—
something of a "gravel" aroma reminiscent of Livermore Valley
wines; finally, an aroma of sweetness, not of honey so much as
raisins. The wine is slightly heady, by comparison with German
Rieslings.

All of these characteristics come across on the palate, full, medium sweet in the mouth and yet clean and refreshing. There is no
remarkable sugar/acid structure; there is *appropriate*, rather than
high, acidity. Whereas the raisin sweetness is only hinted at on
the nose; very fruity, raisiny flavors predominate on the palate
and linger quite insistently on the finish. This is unmistakably a
wine made from botrytised grapes. The *goût de terroir* becomes
more of a background which one gets at the back of the palate.
Absolutely lovely wine.

Joseph Phelps Johannisberg Riesling, 1973, Napa

tasted at one and one half years old

There is a faint green tint in the delicate yellow color of this wine.
On the nose, there is something of the fragrance of Moselle
Spaetlese. There is the flowery aspect of Riesling with a faint
aroma of honey. In the background there is a hint of the Napa
origin of the wine. It is this Napa volcanic background aroma,
kept so perfectly subdued, which makes this in its own way, an
elegant wine (neither the Wente nor the Beringer are what might
be called elegant).

On the palate, the wine is quite dry—this is evidently not a botrytis late-harvest Riesling although the nose might have inclined one to think so. There is, on the other hand, exceptional acidity which opens the palate to an array of delicate flavors. The fruit does not overwhelm the palate. The wine is in absolutely perfect balance, particularly in the way that all the complex aromas come through on the palate. The finish is not insistently fruity; rather, traces of acidity keep nuances of flavor very much alive at the finish. Winemaker Walter Schug has studied and worked in the Rheingau. His mastery of Riesling technique is clearly evident. This is a minor masterpiece, by California standards.

Quite possibly the finest Johannisberg Riesling made in California is this lovely:

Freemark Abbey Edelwein (*Late Harvest Johannisberg Riesling*), *1973, Napa*

tasted at two and one half years old

This wine is a joy. Glowing honey-yellow in color, the wine has the character of some of the very finest French Sauternes and German Beerenauslesen in memory. Less predominantly Riesling in character, the exquisite botrytis character has the upper hand. The bouquet is delicate and sweet and only beginning to show the complexity it will develop over the next several years. On the palate, the wine is very concentrated in flavor; the tiniest sip just fills the mouth. One is reminded of apricots. The wine is perhaps sweeter than a comparable Beerenauslese but there is an exceptional acidity (.92) which keeps the wine alive, refreshing and not at all cloying. This wonderfully delicious wine is only beginning to show its potential.

The wine inspired one of my dinner guests to toss off this charming little sketch which quite admirably expresses the wine:

California Chenin Blanc

Twelve

Most writers mention Vouvray as the French counterpart of California Chenin Blanc. Although Vouvrays are widely distributed, I find that they are the least predictable of French wines in terms of quality—ranging, even in the same vintage, from very fine to abominable. In my own experience, there has been only one California Chenin Blanc, the 1973 of Stonegate (Napa), which bore any distinct resemblance to the wine of Vouvray. Quite honestly, this Stonegate Chenin Blanc is such a lovely dry wine, certainly finer than any Vouvray I have ever tasted, that I hesitate to make the comparison! Brother Timothy's lovely version of Chenin Blanc—Christian Brothers' Pineau de la Loire, Special Cuvée—often has the soft natural sparkle which one occasionally finds in a Vouvray but, here again, the comparison ends at that point.

The really significant French Chenin Blancs and the most appropriate point of comparison are the fine dessert wines of Coteaux du Layon and Quart de Chaume and the lovely dry Chenin Blanc of nearby Saviennières.

The weather conditions along the Loire Valley at Coteaux du Layon are such that they foster the development of the "noble mold", botrytis. These are the conditions which also produce the rich, unctuous dessert wines of Sauternes. There is a major difference, however; the Chenin Blanc vine is naturally prolific. It contributes much less of the concentrated varietal fruit characteristics than the vines which go into the making of Sauternes, viz., Semillon, Sauvignon Blanc and Muscadelle. Being farther north the grapes of the Coteaux du Layon do not generally reach as high a sugar as the more southerly Sauternes vines. The result is a concentrated, honeyed wine, less complex and richly sweet than a Sauternes; rather, somewhere between a Barsac and a Moselle Auslese. The fruit of the wine is reminiscent of sun ripened honeydew melon. Chestnut cooperage adds a very distinct mellowness to the wines.

Chenin Blanc seems to need a fair amount of residual sugar to bring out its delicate ripe melon varietal flavor. It is a variety which, if fermented bone dry, often produces wine with little or no fruit. Even the drier French version, Savennières, is generally not fermented out bone dry. Although fairly dry, a fine Savennières will retain the honey and melon character of its sweeter neighbors.

All of these French Chenin Blancs have a sameness of character and treatment which makes them somewhat predictable—the California version of Chenin Blanc is anything but predictable. In fact, Chenin Blanc has gone through so many different treatments, that one should be ready for both delightful surprises and sad disappointments. Careful, selective buying is very important.

In California, the burgeoning wine market needed a dinner wine which was dry enough to accompany entrees, but sweet enough to tease the emergent American palate into the pleasures of dry dinner wines—a kind of bridge for the naive palate. Chenin Blanc proved to be the perfect answer.

In 1955, Charles Krug (Napa) was the first to introduce a demi-sec Chenin Blanc—the wine created an immediate sensation. This Krug Chenin Blanc was so popular that within a decade several wineries followed with their own demi-sec Chenin Blanc: Christian Brothers, Sebastiani, Robert Mondavi, Wente Brothers (a blend of Chenin Blanc and Trebbiano, the grape of Italian Soave wines), Inglenook, Mirassou, Oakville Vineyards and many others.

Chenin Blanc found a very congenial home in California. It fulfilled a very definite need but beyond that it seemed to develop a lovely fruitiness and charm which made it distinctly and inimitably Californian. Chenin Blanc took on a new identity in California, quite beyond anything that it had in France. Many connoisseurs who approach California wine with a set of European preconceptions have been blinded to the charm of California Chenin Blanc. What a pity!

These demi-sec Chenin Blancs are in an entirely different class and are made in a different style from the French version. There is no honeyed, botrytis character and little or no wood character. They are typically Californian in that all the emphasis is on the fruit, underlined by the residual sugars. They are generally delightful, uncomplicated wines which have become understandably popular. Part of the secret of these wines is the slow, very cool fermentation which most of them undergo. A great deal of fresh fruit character and acidity is retained in controlled fermentation so that, in spite of the sweet edge, they are seldom flat or cloying.

In order to make a demi-sec wine it is generally necessary to sterilize the must toward the end of the fermentation with a small amount of sulfur. This stabilizes the wine and prevents yeast from fermenting the remaining .5% to 2% sugar. In French Chenin Blancs, the wines are often so light-bodied that traces of sulfur often come through very annoyingly. In the California version, the wines have sufficient body and fruitiness that this need not happen, except through clumsy winemaking practice.

Perhaps the finest demi-sec California Chenin Blanc was made at Mirassou in 1970.

Mirassou Chenin Blanc, 1970, Monterey County

tasted at one year old

This wine came from vines planted in the early 1960's at Soledad in Monterey County. The vineyard was planted out to accomodate machine pickers.

The Mirassou Winery is a good sixty miles north of the vineyard; this distance presented a major problem since mechanical picking tends to bruise and cut the fruit. In the case of white wine grapes, this is particularly disadvantageous because spoilage sets in very rapidly. The Mirassous designed some ingenious equipment to go with their mechanical pickers—a device which would stem and crush the fruit on the spot and transfer the must to holding tanks which kept the must both chilled and under a protective cap of carbon dioxide until it reached the winery.

Frosts in the spring of 1970 cut back the productivity of the vines somewhat but the remaining fruit seemed to benefit from the loss of competition. There were also traces of botrytis mold which further concentrated the fruit. The finished wine was an almost perfect expression of the character of the fresh fruit of the grape, semi-dry, utterly luscious and refreshing.

My first acquaintance with this wine came one summer Sunday as I was introducing some east coast guests to the warm hospitality of the Mirassou tasting room in San Jose. The wine was making a great hit with the tasters—it was such an utterly perfect and refreshing wine for a summer day. We purchased a few bottles and, driving south through the lower Santa Clara Valley, we found that it was bell pepper season—large, glossy green peppers were selling at road side stands for two and three cents each; and stewing mushrooms and yellow onions were at incredibly low prices. We could not be restrained. Driving back north through the cool Santa Cruz Mountains, we arrived home and prepared a Lucullan summer feast of chicken sautéed with great quantities of green peppers, mushrooms, onions, and a few cloves of garlic; enriched with demi-glacé (highly concentrated fresh chicken stock) and a bit of wine; and washed down, of course, with our find of the day—Mirassou Chenin Blanc. A perfect summer evening feast.

It is a pity that subsequent vintages have been considerably lesser wines.

Robert Mondavi Chenin Blanc, 1970, Napa

tasted at two years old

Very pale yellow; on the nose, luscious with the ripe melon aroma of Chenin Blanc and a hint of Napa *goût de terroir*, generally more complex, with less of the unabashedly fresh fruit character of the Mirassou. On the palate, somewhat drier, clean, mouthfilling flavors, beautifully balanced. On more than one occasion this made an elegant and refreshing luncheon wine to accompany a Country Pâté en Croute.

Some California Chenin Blancs are made just a bit too sweet for table use, serving rather as nice sipping wines. The 1971 Chenin Blanc of Pedroncelli would be a good example, leaning very much toward Coteaux du Layon in style. Even more successful was:

Gemello Chenin Blanc, Carmel Valley, non-vintage, but most of the grapes were from 1973 vintage

tasted at one and one half years old

In a blind tasting one would be tempted to say Coteaux du Layon in a light year. This wine is from Gemello's new vineyard deep in the Carmel Valley, grown in conditions which are remarkably similar to the Loire Valley. The Carmel Valley narrows to a canyon which cuts through the Coast Range and opens out onto Wente's famous Arroyo Seco vineyards. In many respects, this is a single viticultural complex—Gemello's Chenin Blanc bears a certain kinship with Wente's Arroyo Seco Rieslings.

Light to medium yellow, the wine has a deep, melon-like aroma; there is a certain late-picked character on the nose (evidently there was a considerable amount of botrytis on the grapes) and a hint of wood in the background. The wine is remarkably reminiscent of a Loire Chenin Blanc. Medium dry and very full, fruity and mellow in the mouth with excellent acidity. Lovely wine!

These Monterey County wines made from white grapes which have developed botrytis give only the barest hint of the future glory of this new viticultural region!

Most California winemakers have given a try to making a dry version of Chenin Blanc, with interesting, if extremely mixed, results. Wineries which made both a semi-dry and a dry version tried to avoid confusion by calling their drier version "White Pinot". They did not seem to realize that "White Pinot" is a translation of the French "Pinot Blanc", itself a grape variety which bears no relation whatsoever to Chenin Blanc. Another winery calls *its* drier version "Chenin Blanc" and its sweeter version "Pineau de la Loire", an alternate French term for Chenin Blanc. It takes a while to learn one's way around this comedy of names. Hopefully the label will identify the wine as being either semi-dry or dry, made from Chenin Blanc grapes.

A dry Chenin Blanc is not an easy wine to make. Unlike French Colombard, another prolific but less subtle variety which retains good fruit when it is fermented out very dry; Chenin Blanc is considerably more delicate and requires careful balancing. Several winemakers try to make a bone dry Chenin Blanc, a kind of California equivalent of Muscadet. Unfortunately, "dry" in this case, means merely lacking in residual sugar and not crisp acidity. The only exception that I can think of is the 1972 Chenin Blanc of Stag's Leap Vineyard, Napa Valley. In most other cases the delicate varietal fruit virtually disappears and other curious, earthy flavors crowd in a bit too harshly and obtrusively. One such version strikes me as having an off aroma and flavor of tea leaves. One of the worst offenders is the 1972 White Pinot (dry Chenin Blanc) of Inglenook. This is a totally vapid wine trying to masquerade as a premium wine. I can think of a dozen California jug white wines with more character at a third the price!

One solution is to blend in wine made from the press juice of other premium varietals. This is the practice at Sterling Vineyards where the Chenin Blanc is blended with 30% press wine of Chardonnay. This makes a most attractive wine but relatively little Chenin Blanc character comes through. Such wine might be more appropriately called simply "Napa White"—in the same way that the French use such designations as "Macon

Blanc". Oakville Vineyards makes a similar wine with a different varietal base and uses the charming and appropriate name "Our House Wine"! Theirs is certainly one of the most successful of this type of wine.

Another method is to cut back the productivity of the vines either by hillside plantings or careful pruning. This intensifies the varietal character so that it does not fade out with very little residual sugar. Such a wine is Lee Stewart's dry Chenin Blanc which he calls:

Souverain Cellars "Pineau Souverain", 1971, Napa

tasted at two years old

For me, this was one of Lee's finest wines. Reminiscent of a fine Saviennières, but really in a class by itself. A very pale yellow. On the nose, a lovely flowery bouquet, lots of fruit and an unmistakable background aroma of sage blossom honey—it is difficult to keep one's nose out of the glass!

On the palate, quite dry, with delicate but intense flavors which linger through the excellent finish. A hint of oak compliments the fruit. Excellent acidity, crisp, appetizing and perfectly balanced. This wine made an admirable accompaniment to a carefully prepared Blanquette de Veau. Unfortunately, this wine did not seem to hold its peak over a sufficiently long period of time.

Lyncrest Vineyards Dry Chenin Blanc, 1972, Napa

tasted at two years old

John Henderson, winemaker at Lyncrest, is a protégé of Lee Stewart—the experience is certainly evident in the wine, but the result is very much an expression of his own point of view. Lyncrest Vineyards are high above the valley floor, well up in the Mayacamas Range overlooking the town of St. Helena. These mountain conditions result in a natural check of the productivity of the vines while at the same time producing fruit with both good sugar and high acid. These growing conditions certainly show in the quality of the wine. The delicate melon characteristic of Chenin Blanc is there, framed between an exceptionally good acidity and only enough residual sugar to give definition to the fruit. On the nose, one is reminded of California Chardonnay. But rather than the fullness of Chardonnay in the mouth, it is delicate and refreshing. This wine showed beautifully with Coquilles St. Jacques.

Another fine Chenin Blanc was grown and made in the Mayacamas Range by Bob Travers at Mayacamas Vineyards. Very much in the style of the Lyncrest, this was one of those few California white wines which are excellent with light seafood dishes. I was most disappointed to learn that the Travers have recently pulled up the vines and have replanted the vineyard to another variety of grape.

Chalone Vineyards (Dry) Chenin Blanc, 1971, Monterey County

tasted at four years old

This is a Chenin Blanc which would please and fascinate the most fastidious Burgundian—a dry Loire type wine made in the manner of Meursault! It is another wine made from truly "mountain grown" grapes. A somewhat deeper yellow, the wine looks like a White Burgundy. A very rich but delicate Chenin Blanc nose with a good deal of French Limousin oak character. The fruit and other complexities of bouquet are by no means "covered" by the oak—rather everything is in perfect balance.

On the palate, very dry—meaning superb acid and very little residual sugar. The wine fills the mouth with rich and complex flavors. Because of the exceptional acidity, this wine will hold its peak far longer than either the Souverain or the Lyncrest.

This wine should be thought of in terms of rich, elegant foods, such as roast pheasant, sweetbreads in cream, or perhaps veal scallops with fresh woodland mushrooms.

These few dry Chenin Blancs of great quality should be cause for most other California winemakers to reassess their approach to making a dry wine from this variety.

A Postscript on the Other

California Varietals

Beyond the major premium varietal wines which I have discussed at length, there is a rich assortment of other varietal and generic wines made in California. Many of these wines achieve a high level of quality; but, unfortunately, the majority are made in a perfunctory manner, mainly for the purpose of filling out a product line. Often, one winemaker will hit upon a particularly agreeable and successful interpretation of a varietal. The wine will sell well and other winemakers will jump on the band wagon with less desirable, less carefully thought out versions of the wine at the same, or a higher, price. Often, a varietal wine will experience a sudden vogue and the resulting demand forces the price up beyond reasonable value—a great deal of sifting is necessary. Here, again, a good merchant and some of the current wine letters can be very helpful.

There are many wines in this area which will reward the adventuresome wine lover and the imaginative gourmet. Among the whites, perhaps the most interesting is the varietal *Sauvignon Blanc* (also referred to as Fumé Blanc and Blanc de Sauvignon). This is the one wine which Robert Mondavi Winery (Napa) has made with consistent excellence; although I must say that the 1973 Fumé Blanc (unfiltered) is perhaps their very finest. Ric Forman at Sterling Vineyards (Napa) has taken this varietal very seriously and has made some extraordinary wines. Unfortunately many other Sauvignon Blancs have been lesser wines at prices far higher than is warranted by the quality. Wente Brothers Sauvignon Blanc (Livermore Valley) is an exception. In the 1972 and 1973 vintage, Wente made superb, reasonably priced Sauvignon Blancs which were far superior to many of their overpriced cousins from the Napa Valley. There is something radically wrong when a wine priced in the neighborhood of $2.50 (Wente) is as fine or better than several other wines of the same type priced between $3.50 and $5.00.

It is Professor Amerine's belief that Sauvignon Blanc is the best California white grape variety.[1] This is a controversial point, not without a certain validity. At the present, though, we simply do not have enough fine, reasonably priced Sauvignon Blanc to give this varietal the attention it deserves. The potential is certainly there, and Professor Amerine's opinion might well be borne out at some time in the future.

There are several advantages to the variety Sauvignon Blanc. In California, it retains good acidity. A well made, very dry California Sauvignon Blanc can be particularly appropriate for certain sea food dishes. Sauvignon Blanc has a very interesting varietal character. The best wines are fresh, clean, with an attractive "smoky/flinty" varietal nose. Alexandre Dumas (Dictionary of Cuisine) quotes an 18th century connoisseur of Bordeaux wines who compared this Sauvignon Blanc aroma to the smell of an old carbine. The refreshingly clean, smoky character sets the wine apart, making an interesting contrast to the softer fruitiness of California Chardonnay, Pinot Blanc and Chenin Blanc. The wine does not demand much support from oak so that it should be less costly to make. Perhaps second and third generation oak casks might be used for Sauvignon Blanc as part of a carefully planned ecology of cooperage.

There have been some very nice dry wines made from the variety *Semillon* in California. The wines are generally less austere than Sauvignon Blanc, more richly fruity. To my taste, Concannon (Livermore Valley) has made some of the finest wines from this variety.

Of the Riesling family, some very pleasant, useful wines have been made from the variety *Sylvaner Riesling*. The variety *Gewürztraminer* seems to have more potential for making wines of good character even though the less carefully made California versions are often listless and flabby. Mirassou Vineyards (Santa Clara/Monterey) has lavished special attention on this variety, making some excellent wines in several different vintages. In

---

[1] Journal of the International Wine and Food Society, Vol. I, No. 4 (May, 1975), P. 11.

California, the variety *Grey Riesling* (not a true Riesling but the French Chaucé Gris) makes a wine of little intrinsic interest; but, curiously, the wine seems to come alive very nicely in certain food contexts, with deep-fried sea food or light curry dishes, for example.

San Martin Winery (Santa Clara) has sparked considerable interest in the various *Muscat* varietals with its superb 1973 Moscato di Canelli. This wine won bravos all around the table, served with last year's Thanksgiving turkey. Hank Rubin made a most agreeable suggestion of serving this wine with Cantonese cuisine. Other somewhat sweeter California Muscats (Louis Martini, Charles Krug, Robert Mondavi, Sutter Home, Corti Brothers) can be very nice wines served by themselves at the end of a meal, rather as one might serve a Coteaux du Layon.

There are several other white varietals which can be pleasant wines of no great distinction, uncomplicated wines to suit the unsophisticated palate or to accompany everyday meals. Among them are *French Colombard*, *Green Hungarian*, *Folle Blanche*, and the hybrid varietals *Flora* and *Emerald Riesling*. Here and there among these lesser varietals, experienced wine lovers will come upon an individual wine which makes them sit up and take notice.

Of the reds, a few exceptional wines have been made from the variety *Petite Sirah*; although most of the wines of this variety are quite ordinary, more suitable for blending into standard red table wine. Often, the characteristic black pepper aroma of Petite Sirah, suitable as a background in a blended wine, is overwhelming in a 100% varietal wine.

Most California Petite Sirah vines originated as cuttings taken from Rhône Valley (France) vineyards in the 19th Century. Apparently this variety is no longer planted very widely in the Rhône Valley. The true *Sirah*, the mainstay of today's finest Rhône Wines, has been planted experimentally at Joseph Phelps Vineyards (Napa) and, from all reports, the first wines are showing a great deal of promise.

Concannon (Livermore Valley) was the first to develop Petite Sirah as a successful varietal wine in California. More recently, there have been fine Petite Sirahs made at Ridge, Freemark Abbey, Souverain Cellars and Robert Mondavi, and one of the nicest for the price was made at Mt. Madonna Winery (Santa Clara) in 1969.

Petite Sirah is the one California wine which seems to benefit from an extensive breathing period—the wine should be opened at least eight hours before it is served. Recently, I opened a 1971 Ridge Petite Sirah (York Creek, Napa) a full twelve hours before serving. This was one of the most intensely flavored, complex, beautifully balanced wines in memory—a wine which stood up magnificently to Steak au Poivre.

The varietal *Barbera* has many devotees among connoisseurs of California wine. The wines are usually tart, fruity, full flavored and useful for accompanying hearty, Italian style food.

From the connoisseur's point of view, *Gamay Beaujolais* is perhaps the least interesting California varietal wine. Most of these wines are very light, simple and predictable. They seem to appeal to inexperienced wine drinkers, and serve the legitimate purpose of introducing timid palates to the enjoyment of dry red wine. Occasionally, one will find a Gamay Beaujolais of more than routine interest: among them, those of Sebastiani (Sonoma), Parducci (Ukiah) and Cuvaison (Napa).

The *Napa Gamay* (or simply *Gamay*) is apparently more closely related to the Gamay which is planted in the Beaujolais district of France. It is difficult to compare the two, however, because so many Beaujolais wines are made with the carbonic maceration method, imparting a distinctly different character to the wine. Gamay in California makes a decent enough everyday varietal wine and can also be used very attractively as a blending wine (for example, with Zinfandel and Petite Sirah) to make a basically sturdy, hearty California red table wine. Joseph Swan Vineyards (Sonoma) made a most extraordinary Gamay in 1970, treating it as a top premium varietal. The wine had an incredible flavor intensity, but somehow lacked varietal interest and complexity. Unlike Zinfandel, Gamay does not seem to respond well to such special treatment.

Curiously, some of the best values in California red wine can be found among the generic *Burgundy* or *Claret* wines, but one should not expect these wines to have any strong resemblance to French Burgundy or Bordeaux. The notion that a varietal is necessarily superior to a generic wine is nonsense. Practically speaking, generic wines are blended wines in which no one grape variety predominates. The name merely indicates the degree of dryness (Clarets are relatively dryer than Burgundies, etc.) Some of the older Burgundies of Souverain Cellars (Napa), blended from 50% Zinfandel and 50% Petite Sirah, have developed into extraordinary wines; with six or seven years of age, they are reminiscent of some old, exotically perfumed Rhône wines. This whole area of generic wines is ripe for the discriminating buyer with a limited budget.

Food and California Wine

Thirteen

A few months ago I invited some friends for a tasting of California and Alsatian Gewürztztraminers. For the occasion I prepared a generous quantity of *Choucroute garni*, an Alsatian specialty which combines sauerkraut, bacon, pork, sausage, onions, carrots and potatoes and is perfumed with juniper berry. One of the guests arrived with a dozen brook trout which he had caught that morning. Now trout followed by *Choucroute garni* is certainly as awkward and unlikely a juxtaposition of two dishes as one could imagine. But we were certainly not going to let that small difficulty prevent us from consuming those perfectly fresh little devils.

A lively discussion broke out over the choice of wine for the trout. Would any or all of the Gewürztztraminers do, or should we consider some other wine? One of the guests quoted a winery tour guide who had asserted that one should drink whatever wine one liked with whatever food one liked, that all the hocus-pocus about food and wine was so much nonsense. Being totally averse to this school of thought, I saw the perfect opportunity to put this theory to rest forever. I dug out a couple of bottles of a youngish and very acidic French Petite Chablis which turned out to be absolutely first rate against the trout sauté meuniere. The rich nut brown butter sauce balanced the puckery acidity of the wine and the two acted as a perfect frame to highlight the delicate flavors of the trout.

For the sport of it, we all tried the softest, least acidic and least dry California Gewürztztraminer against the trout. The fish was bad enough, tasting like a piece of old swordfish under the influence of the wine; but the wine turned into a flat and fishy tasting witch's brew, barely palatable against the trout. We kept enough of the Petite Chablis to taste against the sauerkraut. In that context, it was more like taking a mouthful of raw white vinegar. Needless to say, the gentle Gewürztztraminer became an altogether different and marvelous wine when it was tasted with the sauerkraut. One cannot, we concluded unanimously, serve any wine one likes with any food one likes!

There is another school of thought on food and wine which goes off the deep end in the opposite direction. This school recommends only "proper", safe choices according to a dogmatic set of rules: only red wine with red meat, only white wine with white meat, and a whole list of do's and don't's, anything to avoid social embarrassment and the appearance of ignorance. This school addresses itself to the "statistical" American wine drinker who buys only an occasional bottle of wine for a special occasion. It assumes that no ordinary American could possibly enjoy wine as a daily, civilized pleasure, much less understand *why* certain combinations of food and wine are appropriate.

The relationship between food and wine is not as simple as these people would like to think—unless, of course, one chooses to eat unimaginative food accompanied by wines of little character. The situation is difficult, especially for the novice, but it is not hopelessly difficult. With a certain amount of very pleasant experimentation, one can develop an understanding of the interplay of food and wine. The task demands a fair sensitivity to subtle differences but is certainly not beyond the capability of people with good sense and good taste.

There are many wines which have gained a justifiable reputation for being appropriate with certain dishes. Almost any cookbook which deals with classical cuisine will have a guide which lists the classical combinations. Some of the writings of André Simon and Waverly Root are rich with suggestions. One could hardly do better than to experiment with some of the traditionally appropriate combinations of food and wine.

One should seek out a restaurant with a good listing of California wines and a knowledgeable waiter to help one's gastronomic research along. Unfortunately, neither good California wine lists nor knowledgeable waiters are easy to find. Most restaurants have allowed their liquor distributor to take too great a hand in the selections of wines, with the result that most wine lists offer those California wines with the least character and the highest mark-up. When a decent wine is listed, it is generally priced beyond reason. This is probably the result of the mistaken notion that a restaurant breaks even in the kitchen and makes its profit at the bar. To make matters worse, most waiters have nothing further to offer in the way of assistance beyond a simple hedonic judgment—"*I* liked it."

Fortunately, there are a few fine restaurants with good, sensibly priced listings of California wines. Two personal favorites in the San Francisco Bay Area are Chez Panisse in Berkeley and Narsai's in Kensington, but there are others. An astute restaurant reviewer or simple word of mouth will help one seek them out. The Robert Finigan Wine Guide makes regular and candid assessments of restaurant wine lists.

It is not too much to expect one's wine merchant to have an understanding of food and wine. There is no guarantee that *your* range of tastes will have an affinity with *his* range of tastes. This can only be discovered through experience. One can often judge the caliber of a wine merchant by the amount of thought he gives to your problems in gastronomy and the success of his solutions.

One should certainly try to *understand* the rationale behind the more agreeable combinations of food and wine. Many of these are based on traditions which have grown up where the wines are made. The carafe of Sonoma or Mendocino red wine which accompanies your family style Italian or Basque dinner in San Francisco's North Beach is a good example. The wine is so obviously right for the meal as to be a classic. Throughout Italy, the regional wines have a similar and remarkable affinity for the local cuisine. In California, it is traditional to serve your favorite Chardonnay with the Thanksgiving turkey. And, in Paris, there is a tradition of serving a crisp Muscadet with Belon oysters—by no means the only choice, but somehow superbly right. And generally, the price recommends it.

Winemaking traditions have generally grown up along with the cuisine of a region. Neither seems to precede the other. Rather, the nature of local climate offers a range of possibilities for both the wine and the farm products. The two seem to develop side by side under similar conditions in such a way as to complement each other. In addition to these local conditions, the great centers of cuisine exert a strong influence.

The cuisine of the Bordelais has evolved in such a way as to complement the great wines of the district quite elegantly. The tradition of serving tiny, zesty sausages with oysters is exactly the balancing touch which makes the slightly smoky, flavorsome White Graves Wine a perfect accompaniment. Muscadet would be out of place. Fillet of Beef Bordelais is a perfect complement to fine Claret. The velvety, richly flavored wine-sauce and the garniture of poached marrow are the perfect complements to the finely textured wine.

The relative lightness and austerity of fine claret has certainly come under the influence of the British palate, as is evidenced by such Chateau names as Lynch-Bages, Leoville-Barton, Smith-Haut-Lafite. The appropriateness of red Bordeaux for the roasted meats which the English enjoy so much is probably no accident. I doubt whether we would have as fine a range of Bordeaux as we have today were it not for the British. Theirs is a palate which is sensitive to subtle differences; they have both the patience and the cool cellars to mature them properly; and, contrary to popular belief, the British are entirely capable of producing their own special style of "haute cuisine" which rises to the level of the great Bordeaux wines.

Red Burgundy is another case in point. How beautifully a nice fat Nuits St. Georges complements an authentic Boeuf Bourguignonne and the straw pallet of soft ripening cheeses which follows. This is another combination of food and wine which has become classic.

Burgundy is at the center of the great ancient trade axis which links the Mediterranean, through the Rhône Valley and along the Côte d'Or, with

Belgium and Holland. (How fascinating it is to study the play of northern and southern influences in the architecture of Dijon!) While there are great Burgundy cellars in Dijon and Beaune, and a fine cuisine to match, there are also great Burgundy cellars in Lyons to the south and in Brussels and other cities to the north. The fine cuisines of Lyons and Brussels do very special justice to Burgundian wines.

While there are some fine regional specialties in the United States, the cuisine of America is largely a melting pot affair. We do not have the benefit of a highly refined native cuisine which has developed along with the growing of vines and winemaking tradition. But some of our simple, basic food traditions—the backyard barbecue, fried chicken with country gravy, hamburger sandwiches—these are greatly enhanced by a glass or two of good beverage wine.

The greater percentage of wine made in California is basic beverage wine, skillfully blended, not just to achieve uniformity, but to be appropriate in a wide variety of food contexts. These wines are most agreeable accompaniments to everyday meals, and do not present any sort of gastronomical problem. In fact, it is quite amazing how well suited they can be to such a wide variety of foods.

Within the past fifteen years, the American taste in food has become far more sophisticated, experimental, and heterogeneous. Being a melting pot culture, we have a tremendously rich exposure to various "imported", ethnic cuisines—Italian, French, Oriental, Mexican, Indian, etc. Many Americans have learned to adapt and interpret these cuisines in their kitchens. This should not be thought of as slavish imitation; rather, it is an unprejudiced and intelligent assimilation of culinary values which have developed throughout the world. This ability of American "cuisine" to absorb so many far-flung influences gives evidence of the richness of American agricultural resources.

The immense variety of styles in the premium wines of California is certainly a reflection of this state of affairs. Most of these richly varied wines seem to be able to find an appropriate niche in our melting pot cuisine. Fortunately, California wines have not become rigidly stylized. A good many California winemakers are very conscious of quality. They simply make the best wine they know how to make. They are not afraid to follow their own instincts and tastes in matters of style. American gourmets can be thankful for such a rich variety of choices.

Those California wines which have a great deal of character and individuality, want special food contexts. Being highly individual, there are contexts in which they will show poorly and others in which they will show beautifully. On this level, the winemaker has said, "to hell with product uniformity; let's simply make the very best wine that we can possibly make." Wines of the same maker are often markedly different in different vintage years. (The old saw that California wines are the same year in and year out, is true for some wines because they are *blended* to be that way.) There are simply no pat answers, no backlog of tradition which will define their place on the table. The consumer is forced to become imaginative and inventive in finding contexts which do justice to these fine wines.

As a beginning, one might experiment by making substitutions of California wines in the formulas which tradition has developed for European wines. For example, *California Pinot Noir* = *Nuits St. Georges*, ergo, serve it with Beef Bourguignonne; or *California Cabernet Sauvignon* = *Red Bordeaux*, ergo serve it with Fillet of Beef Bordelais.

As an ultimate rule, this kind of substitution breaks down very quickly. Finer California wines deserve a more careful, more reflective pairing-off with fine food.

In California, we have been forced to re-think the entire relationship between food and wine. We need an understanding of this relationship which goes beyond traditional formulas. Matching food and wine is basically an artistic judgment—what one is trying to achieve is a special degree of overall balance and harmony.

Experimentation, cumulative experience and personal taste form the bases of most sound judgments which match food and wine. It is extremely difficult to rationalize these judgments; and it would certainly be unwise to develop anything further than a few general guidelines. The experimental attitude (or at least open mindedness) should be maintained, for much of the enjoyment of matching food and wine is derived from the element of surprise and discovery.

In the remainder of the chapter, I offer a few guidelines which I have found useful. They form a kind of rudimentary aesthetic or philosophy of food and wine. I try to develop a general attitude toward food and wine which will help one in understanding their interrelationship and form a basis for experimentation. My approach is personal and is based on reflections I have made on the peculiarly difficult problem of matching California wines of special character and quality with appropriate foods. Some of the wines are so inimitable and fine that one is almost forced to take a broader point of view; in fact, some of the wines are of such quality that there is no need whatsoever to take a defensive, narrowly chauvinistic attitude.

For many people, food (including wine) is a matter of simple, un-reflective likes and dislikes. Food, however, is not a purely hedonistic affair—it is *nourishment, sustenance.* In spite of denials to the contrary, the human metabolism seems to crave a certain balance of nourishment; and people seek this balance, in spite of a consciously hedonistic attitude. Even the slightest degree of reflection convinces most people that nourishment takes precedence over gratification of one's simple food preferences.

There is a sense of well-being connected with the simple animal response to receiving good nourishment from food. When nourishment is recognized as a value which must be secured through control of the environment and the buildup of tradition, food becomes an aspect of general culture and the sense of well-being derived from food forms the basis of aesthetic enjoyment.

Food (and in most cases food and wine specifically) has always had a sacramental character—"breaking bread" with someone has been a basic image of shared well-being and harmony among family and friends. Even burnt sacrifices of food and wine in ancient cultures represented a desire for harmony of relationship between man and gods. Dionysius, the Greek god of wine, was something of a salvation figure who mediated between man and gods, intensifying the harmony of relationship. Food graced with fine wine has always been a great catalyst for intensifying and enriching human relationships. What a pity it has taken Americans so long to make this discovery!

The *aesthetic* character of food and wine should not be considered in abstraction from either its *nutritional* character or its *social* character.

Most of our more complete, nutritionally balanced food experiences, whether they include wine or not, have a fundamental structure. First, there are basic protein-nutritional constituents in the ensemble of foods: meats, fish, vitamins, minerals, etc.; second, there are basic and immediate sources of energy: fats, oils, sugars, starches, fruit and vegetable carbohydrates, alcohol. There is a natural and immediate craving for energy felt in the pang of hunger (starches, sugars and other energy foods assuage hunger very quickly but not with total satisfaction). Third, there are types of piquancy which are neither basic sources of nourishment nor sources of energy. They function as inducements to appetite: spices, salt, vinegars, citric juices and wine acidity. These enhance the appetite, stimulate the flow of saliva and gastric juices necessary for digestion, and counteract the appetite dampening effect of the energy foods. Properly integrated, these fundamental types of food value create nutritional balances which lay the foundation for aesthetic balance in foods. It is when these fundamental types of food value are consciously and artfully integrated so that they achieve not only nutritional balance, but also an overall harmonious effect on human sensibilities, that food, or food and wine, can be considered to have aesthetic character and balance. Let me give a wide range of examples which will illustrate my basic thesis.

Consider wine itself as a food, in the light of this concept. The three basic food values cut right across the makeup of wine. There are health giving fruit extracts, minerals and vitamins; there are energy giving sugar and alcohol; and there is appetite provoking acidity. Sweet wine, for example, tends to be a complete experience, often calling for nothing other than itself. A glass of port or Madeira on a winter afternoon provides warming energy food (sugar and alcohol), rich, health giving extract, and enough acidity to keep the sweetness from cloying; or at the end of the meal, the sweetness of fine port or Madeira forms a kind of final punctuation to what has gone before—the sweetness completes one's appetite.

Consider a wine for a summer afternoon. Here, one wants thirst quenching refreshment, a wine which has a sweet enough edge to make it complete in itself, but not so sweet as to inhibit drinking it as a thirst quenching beverage. A demi-sec California Chenin Blanc can often be perfect in this context.

The *acidity* and *lack of sugar* in a *dry* wine, however, *stimulates* the appetite. Without sugar to balance or depress the appetite, it wants food. Perhaps the most successful *table* wines are those which make one think immediately of food!

Consider the opening example of California Gewürztraminer and garnished sauerkraut: do not look at the wine as a separate *object* versus the food as an *object*. Consider the overall food/wine *experience* according to the three basic food values. Here, the sauerkraut, rather than the wine, provides the acidity which is needed to make the ensemble of food and wine appetizing. The *spiciness* of the wine, rather than its acidity, provides an additional supporting and appetizing effect. The residual sugar and alcohol in the wine, the potato, the pork and bacon fats and cooking oils form the energy based constituents of the ensemble. Together, they mollify the acidic impact of the sauerkraut, forming a balancing framework for the protein/nutritional content of meats, vegetables and wine extract. Here is an ensemble which is at once appetizing, nutritious and aesthetically pleasing.

On a very primitive level, consider the typical American who smothers his hamburger and grease laden french-fried potatoes with catsup. The acetic acid in the catsup is necessary to balance all that grease! Here is food which is virtually all framework with very little actual nutritional content. A nice, full, refreshing red jug wine from the central valley would be a far better source of acidity than the blanket of catsup. The honest, wholesome character of the wine, though, might show up the miserable wafer of meat and the spongy, flavorless roll. One would want a substantial, good quality beef patty and chewy, flavorsome french or sour dough bread to give balance and wholesomeness which, in its small way, has an aesthetic appeal.

Chinese cuisine has a word for the overall aesthetic harmony of foods in ensemble. The word *tom* is one of those oriental concepts which is an identity of opposites—*tom* is an absence of flavor and at the same time the intricate balance created by the complex interplay of flavors, aromas and textures. Orientals use this identity of opposites to express the insubstantial character of flavor, the way flavors blend and counter-blend with other flavors. Orientals have never burdened themselves with the westerner's rigid distinction between subject and object. They have a special sensibility for understanding how foods blend and are contrasted in our immediate experience. They do not look at foods as substantial objects. There is a great deal to be learned from their point of view, particularly in the way that we experience and enjoy the interplay of food and wine.

Chinese cuisine is thought out with very keen aesthetic and nutritional good sense. There are intensities and juxtapositions of texture and flavor: the crunchy texture and sweet exuding juice of undercooked snow peas against tender nuggets of meat from the breast of chicken. There are sudden punctuations of appetizing spice: fresh coriander or thin slices of fresh ginger root. There is the soft texture and low flavor profile of rice which absorbs and communicates other flavors. There is a dish which includes nuggets of pork, pineapple and crisp green pepper and onion framed in a sauce which includes the opposites of sweet and acid. And there are sharp outlines created by pungent sauces. Fine oriental soy sauces are often made with as much care as fine wine. The dry, slightly tannic edge of tea provides a certain appetite provoking acidity and does not interfere with the occasional punctuation of sweetness. Here, one can discern the complex interplay of the three basic food values, so carefully balanced that wine is often an immodest intrusion.

In the remainder of the chapter, I will discuss the three food value groups (first, the appetite provoking group; second, the protein/nutritional group; and third, the energy group) particularly with a view to the effect their interaction has on our sensibilities, and with close attention given to the manner in which I use this scheme to match fine California wine with food.

Wine acidity has several very important functions. It acts as a preservative in wine, retarding oxidation and spoilage; and, as we have noted earlier, it has a very important effect on the palate. It opens up not only the palate but the olfactory sensors as well so that one can appreciate the more subtle flavor elements. Wine acidity not only brings out subtleties of flavor in the *wine*, especially on the finish, but it brings out subtle nuances of flavor in foods. This is why the crisp acidity of a fine Hanzell, Mayacamas, or Chappellet Chardonnay is so appropriate for very delicate and refined fish dishes. The acidity plays up the subtle flavors of the fish. The wine is intensely and elegantly flavored but not so full-bodied as to overwhelm the fish.

It is not sufficient that a dry wine be simply lacking in sweetness. It should have the positive presence of an attractive acidity in order to be a good food wine. Acidity plays the very important role of delaying the digestive action of saliva so that foods and wines can come across the palate with their flavors intact, without their being prematurely transformed and partially digested by saliva before they can be fully savored.

A good, dry acidic wine is not only appetite inducing; it is, quite literally, mouth watering. Because acidity inhibits the immediate action of saliva, it induces the flow of additional saliva to compensate for its protective and inhibitive action. This, of course, should not be understood to imply that acidity inhibits digestion. The very opposite is the case. Wine acidity induces an abundant flow of gastric juices so that food accompanied by a dry wine is far more easily and thoroughly digested than food without wine.

Acetic acid (vinegar) plays much the same role. The right amount of vinegar in a salad, balanced and softened in its astringency by fine oil, opens up the palate to the delicate flavor of the greens. A simple salad is a completely balanced, self-contained dish; it does not need (in fact it fights) additional acidity from wine.

Vinegar provides both acidity and flavor to salad. The *quality* of vinegar in salad is very important. For years, Dino Barengo made probably the finest, most flavorful California red wine vinegar. The vinegar was aged very patiently in oak so that there was a substantial loss in volume, but great intensification of flavors derived from the wine and oak. Hopefully, the new owners of Barengo Cellars (Lodi) will not compromise this time consuming method.

Wine is not an attractive accompaniment to simple salad. On the other hand, a complex salad, which includes, say, avocado and shrimp or crab meat, can be a fine *plat* for a richly flavored, but nicely acidic, California Chardonnay. I am thinking of some of the more recent Chardonnays of Spring Mountain and Cuvaison. The rich mellowness of the avocado is an interesting complement to these nicely full Napa Chardonnays.

Highly spicy food provides the necessary appetite provoking elements to make a wine of good acidity unnecessary and perhaps jarring. The piquancy of Mexican pepper sauces and Indian curries induces the flow of saliva and gastric juices and balances the starches. A simple, thirst quenching beverage is desired—for curry, beer or a simple but assertive California white (such as Wente Grey Riesling) would be good. Mexican food wants the slight bitterness of thirst quenching Mexican beers; however, domestic (U.S.) beers are often too filling. A well chilled beverage rosé from the central valley (the drier version generally called "Pink Chablis") would be superior.

A somewhat less piquant and more complex Spanish *paella* wants sangria or perhaps a very fruity, drier, more complex Zinfandel rosé from Mayacamas (Napa) or Pedroncelli (Sonoma). In general, the more piquant the dish, the more any complexity in the wine will become imperceptible.

White wines with high acid are fairly rare in California, making it difficult to select wine for very delicate fish entrees (e.g., raw oysters or trout meunière). By making adjustments (e.g. oysters Rockefeller or trout amandine) one might select a Robert Mondavi Fumé Blanc or a Sauvignon Blanc from Spring Mountain (both Napa) or Wente Brothers (Livermore).

Acidity and piquancy are only a third of the picture. The actual flavor extract constituents of wine should be balanced with the flavor elements in foods. The fullness of extract in red wine is needed to balance the fullness of flavor extract in cheeses and the juices of red meat which is less than well-done.

In general, wines and foods should "stand-up" to each other. Each course in a meal has an overall flavor profile with its own level of assertiveness. A course might be complete on its own or call for a wine with appropriate flavor assertiveness to complement the foods.

Various wines and foods have similar levels of assertiveness but varying degrees of complexity. Generally, simple foods want simple wines; complex foods want complex wines. Neither assertiveness nor complexity can be measured, and no amount of formula making can replace actual experience and familiarity with both foods and wines.

In the chapter on wine tasting, I recommended that the less experienced wine lover should experiment with serving two wines with the same entree. This not only gives valuable perspective for comparing the *wines*, but it also gives a valuable perspective on the peculiar affinities which certain wines have for certain foods. A lesser wine might well be a superior match for an entree because both food and wine have similar levels of intensity and sophistication, while the greater complexity and delicacy of the superior wine might be overpowered by its awkward context. For example, one lesser white wine might be perfect for your chicken and dumplings while the superior white is making you think of something far more elegant, far more refined which would show off the wine.

It is important, as I have already mentioned, to taste a great many wines with a view to estimating their *utility* at table, to get beyond the preoccupation with scoring and ranking wines.

Once it is in the bottle, a wine is a *fait accompli*, nothing can be added or taken away. One can only change the character of the wine by leaving it alone to age and develop on its own in the bottle.

Food is a different matter. The flavor profile of foods is relative and can be adjusted from gentle authority to outright dominance either by adding or taking away.

Traveling up the Italian peninsula, it is fascinating to watch the subtle transformations which the pasta course undergoes and the simple adjustments which are made to accommodate the flavor profile of the food to the local wine which accompanies it.

In the far south, there is an abundance of spaghetti, hot and spicy sausages, zesty, acidic tomato sauce made with generous quantities of herbs, garlic and olive oil. The red *vino di tavola* is pungent with the acidity and tannic bite of very young wine. Here is wine which "stands up" to the dominating assertiveness of the pasta, rather like the ebullient, gesticulatory conversation which is part of the conviviality of the southern Italian table. All that wine acidity and sauce acidity is necessary to keep the starch and oil from dampening one's appetite prematurely. How else could one pack away all that pasta?!

In California, one might prepare the same richly flavored spaghetti and serve a Barbera from Giumarra (Central Valley) or a jug red from Kenwood (Sonoma) or Gemello (Santa Clara). The rich assortment of these California jug wines is phenomenal! I mention these specifically because they are personal favorites—there are many others which would do equally well.

At Naples, there is a soft, gently fruity, local white wine of volcanic aroma which is so delicious that one can hardly stop drinking it. The portion of *al dente* spaghetti is smaller and of impeccable quality and flavor. There are several baby clams in the shell, a few sautéed, tiny fresh tomatoes, and fine olive oil. The scant spoonful of clam broth marries nicely with the oil.

Here, the quantity of starch and oil has been diminished to accomodate the softer acidity of the wine. The gentle assertiveness of the wine matches the flavor profile of the clams, the broth, the oil and the pasta while the tiny whole tomatoes provide an interesting punctuation of acidity. These are simple, clearly drawn and beautifully balanced contrasts. In California, one would find a comparable wine in a two to three year old Pinot Blanc or Dry Semillon from Wente Brothers (Livermore).

At Florence, one is served a fairly small portion of light, freshly made egg noodles—*fettuccine*. The sauce is rich with meat and finely minced vegetables, with a background of tomato, and there is an abundance of freshly grated cheese. The wine is a richly flavored but zesty Chianti Classico.

Here, the starch in the pasta is lightened with egg so that it does not demand as clearly defined a contrast in acidity. The richly complex flavors of sauce and cheese compliment the greater complexity of the wine. In California, a good selection for this type of dish might be a Cabernet of a fairly light year; for example, Inglenook, 1967 (Napa, regular bottling) or a Zinfandel made in the Italian style from Corti Brothers (Amador County) or Kenwood (Sonoma, Special Bin). One might even select a fine jug Zinfandel from the Valley of the Moon Winery (Sonoma), a jug Claret from D'Agostini (Sierra foothills), or jug Cabernet from Italian Swiss Colony.

The principle of balancing the flavor assertiveness between food and wine takes precedence over the "rule"—red wine with red meat, white wine with white meat. In fact this "rule" can be quite safely forgotten. Take, for example, the huge 1972 Chardonnay of Mt. Eden Vineyards (Santa Clara). By 1977-78, this wine will be ready to accompany a medium-rare fillet of beef Wellington—so incredibly rich in fruit and oak extract is this wine! Boiled beef, in which much of the extract is cooked out of the beef and into the broth, wants a wine with lighter extract, even a very positively flavored California Johannisberg Riesling would do nicely.

Must one serve a white wine with fish? A fine rosé from Souverain of Alexander Valley (Sonoma) or Burgess Cellars (Napa) would be excellent for Bouillabaise, or Sacramento River crayfish in a Bordelaise type sauce. A nice firm Rex sole in a Mournay sauce would provide enough flavor assertiveness (particularly from the cheese) to suit a very light, *very* dry red wine, a California Gamay Beaujolais or a light Zinfandel or perhaps the white wine made from Pinot Noir at Caymus Vineyards (Napa). If there is a fair amount of residual sweetness in the wine, the sugar, it seems, picks up the fish extracts and the wine will have a fishy taste.

One of the most surprising red-wine-with-fish combinations was a dry, medium-full and very fruity Zinfandel of Louis Martini 1971 (Napa) which accompanied Mandarin steamed fish. In the preparation of this dish, diagonal incisions are made in the flesh of a whole striped bass at regular intervals. Wafer-thin slices of fresh ginger root are inserted. The fish is scattered with slivered scallion tops and is steamed in a closed container with only enough water to give a cup or so of broth. The steaming completed, the broth is enriched with sesame seed oil and a slightly sweet soy sauce. The flavor of ginger so permeates the tender white flesh and the broth is so appropriately assertive that the flavor profile of the dish is raised to a level where it copes beautifully with the red wine.

The *energy* based group in food and wine (oils, fats, alcohols, sugars, starches) all have an important relation to flavor extract and assertiveness. The chemistry of the matter is very complex and, quite honestly, I do not strive for scientific accuracy of statement. What I have to say is based solely on personal experience. The *sensory, aesthetic* effect of the relationship between the energy group and other foods can be quite simply stated and verified. These energy forms are quite neutral in flavor, except, of course, the *taste* of sugar. But they all have the special ability to absorb flavor and odor elements into their structure, making these extracts particularly accessible to the sense of taste and smell. A range of examples should help to make my meaning clear.

Fats, butterfats and *oil* seem to have a special capacity to absorb flavor extracts. Oil is a medium for scents and essences (e.g., oil of clove). The scent and flavor of orange and lemon is naturally present in the oils at the surface of the skin (the zest). The French make extensive use of flavored butters (lobster, shallot, herb, etc.), and most cooks know that when an unpeeled clove of garlic is tossed in hot oil for a couple of minutes, the flavor of garlic will permeate and perfume the oil. Fats and oils seem to act as flavor conductors.

Animal fat has long been recognized as a source of flavor in meats. For this reason well-marbled beef is thought to be more richly flavored. Fillet of beef is perhaps the leanest cut and is also the lowest in flavor profile. Fillet which has been larded with strips of fat has a great deal more flavor. Exactly *why* this is so seems to be a matter of controversy. It is perhaps safe to say that the interplay of lean meat with a proper proportion of fat gives the richest flavor on the palate.

Meats and other foods which are rich in fats and oils seem to put the acidity of a very dry wine in too high relief. A bridge is needed by way of a trace of residual sugar or a sweet finish to the wine from glycerol. Burgundian cuisine makes liberal use of pork fat lardoons to give richness of tone to meat dishes prepared *à la Bourguignonne*. This is done to balance the residual sweetness which is characteristic of red Burgundy. The cuisine of the Bordelais tends to underplay the role of fats and oils in meat preparation, in order to accomodate the relative austerity of Claret. Well aged California Cabernets seem to lie somewhere in between. They are particularly appropriate for richly marbled, well flavored American beef. Being somewhat less complex than either red Bordeaux or red Burgundy, they do not need meat preparations which entail elaborate embellishment—simpler preparations are more appropriate. Provided the meat and the wine are of the finest quality, the combination of well aged California Cabernet and simple roasted or grilled American beef can deliver gastronomic enjoyment of the highest order.

California Cabernet is particularly fine with grilled or roasted lamb. Because sheep are pasture fed and not grain fed, there is perhaps a slight gamy flavor which some people find objectionable. California Cabernet provides just the right edge of fruitiness and the barest trace of residual sweetness to cut through this slight gaminess. I personally feel that it is a waste to serve fine red Burgundy with lamb (although I would get plenty of argument here) and fine red Bordeaux is often a shade too light for most preparations of lamb. A little gastronomic experimentation should settle the question according to personal taste.

Cheeses which have a high butterfat content will make a light, dry red wine seem unattractively acid. Medium-butterfat cheese such as Gouda, Swiss or Port Salut would be more appropriate for such wine (e.g., a lighter Zinfandel). Fermented cheese with high butterfat (Brie, Camembert, etc.) wants a red wine with complexity and some residual sweetness such as French Red Burgundy. California Pinot Noir is almost invariably less complex than French Pinot Noir, but it is admirable with some of our domestic soft ripening cheese such as *Rouge et Noir* brand which is proportionately less complex than French cheese of the same type. I am thinking here of the Caymus Vineyards Pinot Noir 1972 or the Stonegate Pinot Noir 1973, both very fine Napa Pinot Noirs. These lighter Pinot Noirs are also superb with *Tripes à la Mode de Caen*. The tendency of California Cabernets and the heavier Zinfandels to be rich in fruit makes them first-rate wines to accompany both the main entree and a cheese course which follows immediately. The pungent flavors of the cheese seem to bring out the special and unique fruitiness of these California reds.

White wines which are rich in fruit and oak extract and are not bone dry want appropriately rich food contexts: fish or veal or chicken sauced in a *velouté* enriched with cream and butter. The cream and butter enrichment gives the sauce a lush texture and gives the dish itself greater complexity. The additional richness which the oak contributes to the wine is balanced by the additional richness which the cream and butter contribute to the sauce. There is a wide range of California Chardonnay, Pinot Blanc, Dry Chenin Blanc, along with some Johannisberg Rieslings and Sauvignon Blancs which can be put in this context. Various adjustments can be made in the sauce to accommodate the flavor level of the wine: thinning with stock or milk, balancing the richness with a squeeze of lemon, further enrichment with egg yolks, sharpening with a touch of curry, etc. All thickened sauces have the very important function of coating morsels of solid food, raising their intensity and complexity of flavor. Meats, fish or poultry in thinner sauces or broths tend to have a lower, less complex profile. Flavors tend to be separated and contrasted, wanting a simpler, less rich wine which acts as one of the elements in the contrast. I am thinking here of Sylvaner, Grey Riesling and Dry Semillon. These latter are also appropriate for simple sautés and some deep-fried foods (provided the oil is of good condition and quality).

Cantonese stir-fry foods present an interesting problem. Morsels of vegetables and meat are stirred and quickly fried in a small amount of oil and then braised very briefly. A light binding of diluted cornstarch fuses the oil with whatever juices have exuded from the meats and vegetables. This makes a sauce which clings to the morsels of food, gently intensifying their flavors and acting as a subtle flavor conductor. In stir-fried vegetables and beef, there is a gentle tannic bite to the undercooked vegetables and a sweet and pungent note contributed by soy sauce. The tannic edge in the tea which usually accompanies it provides the right acidic balance against the oil and the touch of sweetness in the sauce. This presents the difficult problem of a choice of wine to replace the tea. The fruitiness of most wine is an extraneous note to the well integrated flavors and textures of the dish. One might try a very austere white wine, very low in residual sugar, but not, on the other hand, highly acidic, a wine with a bite to it, a *goût de terroir*. I am thinking here of a young Dry Chenin Blanc from Chappellet (Napa) or Dry Creek Vineyards (Sonoma).

In experimenting with wine and oriental food, it is perhaps advisable to have several people at table so that different wines can be served with several different dishes, making interesting cross comparisons and intriguing cross-currents of flavor.

Alcohol has traditionally been the medium for scent and perfume essences and for such food extracts as vanilla and almond. The aromatic character of wine is partially based on flavor elements in the wine which become infused into the alcohol during fermentation, barrel aging and bottle aging. It is the volatile nature of alcohol, along with what oenologists call esters and aldehydes, which makes these flavor elements accessible to the olfactory sense in bouquet. The relative strength of alcohol in a wine has a distinct effect on the flavor elements in the wine, its aroma, and the flavor of foods which it accompanies. A wine with higher alcohol content (say 13%–15%) softens the astringency of its own acid content and gives the wine a richer texture. Such a wine seems to be able to absorb more oak flavor without being thrown off balance.

Against foods, a high alcohol wine will mollify acidic or strongly flavored elements in foods. A wine with moderate extract assertiveness but high alcohol will do well with Duck à l'Orange, perhaps a rich California Chardonnay with something in the neighborhood of 14% alcohol. Here, the alcohol softens the pungently acidic character of orange while the extract is moderate enough to highlight the flavors of the duck. In an even more difficult situation, a fairly high alcohol, dry Johannisberg Riesling from Freemark Abbey (Napa) would be interesting against Peking Duck with pungent *hoisin* sauce. Consider, for example, the 1972 Chardonnay of Montelena (made from a blend of Napa and Alexander Valley grapes). The wine is bright yellow, richly fruity on the nose with only the barest hint of oak. The wine is 13.2% alcohol, giving a soft, clean and very full Chardonnay character on the palate with an interesting *goût de terrior* and a slightly citric finish. This wine was a particular favorite which I have served in several different food contexts. It was perhaps at its best against Veal Picata: thin slices of veal, dusted in flour and sautéed very quickly in butter and oil and then flamed with a small amount of domestic white port. The scallops of veal are removed to a serving platter and arranged with alternating wafer thin cartwheel slices of lemon. Meanwhile, there is some rich veal stock reducing in the sauté pan under high fire to make a rich but uncomplicated sauce for the veal. The white port keeps the sauce only slightly sweet (appropriate to the wine) while the veal stock adds depth of flavor to match the rich Chardonnay (for a lesser wine one might have dispensed with the stock). The lemon acidity compensates for the softness of acidity in the wine while the slightly higher percentage of alcohol in the wine keeps the lemon from intruding too aggressively. The delicate flavor of the veal is nicely set off by the other carefully balanced flavors.

One might adjust the basic recipe to accommodate a medium-full, fruity Zinfandel with several years of bottle age in the following manner: adjust the butter/oil to olive oil, add a bit of ground pepper and thyme to the flour, toss in two or three unpeeled cloves of garlic to sauté with the veal, and flame the meat with a good Madeira rather than the port. And rather than the lemon slices, perhaps just a squeeze of lemon juice and chopped parsley.

A very alcoholic, assertively flavored red wine such as the 1973 Ridge Zinfandel (Geyserville) or the 1969 Trentadue "Burgundy" (15% alcohol) would soften the impact of strong flavors in venison or shish-kebab of marinated lamb. Big Zinfandels in the style of the 1973 Ridge are particularly fine with steaks which have been charcoal broiled and brushed with soft butter and a squeeze of lemon. Extremely pungent and flavorful cheddars want an even more highly alcoholic accompaniment such as Ficklin Port (Madera, California). A dry wine with low alcohol tasted against strong cheese, will be disagreeably acidic.

Perhaps the most overlooked role of alcohol in wine is its ability to pick up flavor extracts in foods, making a very subtle transformation in the character of the wine. This is one of the reasons why a wine will taste different against different foods and then still different when tasted alone.

In general, it is unwise to try to rationalize the relationship between food and wine too thoroughly. Hopefully, the guidelines which I have mentioned will not be interpreted too rigidly. Rather, they might be used as points of departure, as hypotheses for gastronomic experimentation. Personal taste, and not what one interprets as socially correct, should prevail. Matching food and wine can be a genuinely creative and satisfying artistic activity which any civilized person can enjoy.

Unfortunately, Americans have been conditioned to think of wine as just another alcoholic beverage (as though a scotch and soda might accompany your roast beef just as well!) The entire attitude toward wine, from production, to marketing, to consumption, to legal control, tends to assume that wine is primarily an alcoholic beverage.

But wine is only incidentally an alcoholic beverage. Wine is primarily an agricultural product, a *food* which plays an integral role in the art of the table. It not only provides energy, nourishment, and the zest which provides healthy appetite, it provides an excellent means by which the body makes efficient use of all its sources of nourishment.

In addition, wine gives us an inexhaustible variety of bouquet and flavor, appealing to our higher sensibilities. Wine challenges and promotes the development of our critical faculty, our aesthetic sensibility and enjoyment.

But perhaps most important of all, wine provides the setting and the stimulus for some of the most intensely rich communications between human beings. Sharing food and wine with family and friends not only sustains, but celebrates life.

It is ridiculous, then, to think of wine as a beverage for the elite or as something which one saves for a special occasion as a matter of social necessity.

Wine is a complex entity; not a standardized and mechanical product, but an individual and richly varied art form which can be shared by all. It ranks among our most cherished cultural values.

Suggestions for Further Reading

Among the books which deal with general wine topics, perhaps the two best are: *Wine: an Introduction for Americans*, by M. A. Amerine and V. L. Singleton (Berkeley: University of California Press, 1965) and *Wine*, by Hugh Johnson (newly revised edition, New York: Simon and Schuster, 1975). Alexis Lichine's monumental *Encyclopedia of Wines and Spirits* (New York: Knopf, 1974) and Frank Schoonmaker's *Encyclopedia of Wine* (5th edition; New York: Hastings House, 1973) are both very helpful. There are some very interesting, if somewhat mystical, general comments on wine in the book by Edouard Kressman, *Wonder of Wine* (New York: Hastings House, 1968).

On the science and technology of wine, there are three classic texts: *Table Wines* by M. A. Amerine and M. A. Joslyn (second edition; Berkeley and Los Angeles: University of California Press, 1970); *Technology of Wine Making* by M. A. Amerine, H. W. Berg and W. V. Cruess (second edition; Connecticut: Avi, 1967) and *General Viticulture* by A. J. Winkler (Berkeley and Los Angeles: University of California Press, 1962).

Among the books on California wine, there are several which deal primarily with the background of the various wineries. *Melville's Guide to California Wines*, by Jeff Morgan (fourth revised edition, San Carlos, California: Nourse Publishing Co., 1972) and *McCall's Guide to Wines of America* by William E. Massee (New York: McCall, 1970) are both very useful. Nathan Chroman's *Treasury of American Wines* (New York: Rutledge-Crown, 1973) is a pleasure to look at and read. *California Wineries, Volume One: Napa Valley* (Vintage Image, 1974) by Michael Topolos and Betty Dopson, includes some important background information on the newer wineries of the Napa Valley. Of the books which describe and discuss specific California wines, *The Fine Wines of California* by Hurst Hannum and Robert S. Blumberg (revised edition; New York: Doubleday, 1973) is very useful. Some of the most enlightening comments and tasting notes and some of the most pleasurable reading on California wines are included in several of Harry Waugh's fine books: *Bacchus on the Wing* (London: Wine and Spirit Publications, 1966), *Pick of the Bunch* (London; Wine and Spirit Publications, 1970), and *Diary of a Winetaster* (New York: Quadrangle Books, 1972). Of the various travel guides to California wine country, the best is still *California Wine Country* (Sunset Books).

For broad, general background and history of wine in California, Leon Adams' *Wines of America* is indispensable. Of the earlier books on California wine, *American Wines*, by Frank Schoonmaker and Tom Marvel (New York: Duell, Sloan and Pearce, 1941), is very interesting, particularly the discussion of the problem of federal and state laws which govern wine distribution. Idwal Jones' *Vines in the Sun* (New York: William Morrow, 1949) is still a great pleasure to read. Certainly the most interesting book on California wines in the 19th century is *Wines and Vines of California* by Frona Eunice Wait (facsimile edition with an introduction by M. A. Amerine; Berkeley: Howell-North Books, 1973). Clarence E. Edwords' *Bohemian San Francisco* (originally published in 1914; facsimile edition, Berkeley: Silhouette Press, 1973) is an intriguing look at the gastronomic world of San Francisco before Prohibition.

On the subject of wine tasting, Michael Broadbent's *Wine Tasting: a practical handbook on tasting and tastings*, (revised edition; London: Christie Wine Publications, 1973) is indispensable. *Modern Sensory Methods of Evaluating Wine* by M. A. Amerine, E. B. Roessler and F. Filipello (Berkeley: University of California Press, 1959) is an important work which should be read along with Professor Amerine's essay on the aesthetics of food and wine, *Flavor as a Value* (footnote, page 31) for a balanced view.

On the subject of geography and its influence on wine, Hugh Johnson's *World Atlas of Wine* (New York: Simon and Schuster, 1971) is richly rewarding and one of the most handsome, functional wine books ever printed.

There are some interesting discussions of food and wine in Hugh Johnson's *Wine* and Edouard Kressman's *Wonder of Wine*. The *Melville*

Guide to California Wines has a very useful list of suggestions for matching food and California wine. Henry Rubin has written a fine essay on food and wine for the magazine *Bon Appétit* (Vol. 17, #4, July-August, 1972). The writings of André Simon are rich with discussions of food and wine. A personal favorite among his works is *The Art of Good Living* (London: Constable, 1929). Waverley Root's *The Food of France* (New York: Knopf, 1970) and *The Food of Italy* (New York: Knopf, 1972) are both fascinating studies in the culture of food and wine. Alexandre Dumas' *Dictionary of Cuisine* (edited, abridged and translated by Louis Colman; London: Spring Books, 1958) is certainly one of the most interesting and enjoyable books ever written on food and wine. Some of the best discussions of food and wine are in a series of articles which appeared in *Wine Magazine* (London: Wine and Spirit Publications) in the early 1970's entitled "Will You Dine Out With Our Master of Wine?". Michael Broadbent is the master of wine, in association with Luke Bayard and Lawrie Strangman. There is a wealth of insight in these articles.

For some of the wine literature which is difficult to find, there are three fine wine libraries in central California: the wine library at the St. Helena (Napa Valley) Public Library, the wine library at the Wine Museum (Fisherman's Wharf, San Francisco), and an extensive collection of rare wine books and literature at the University of California at Davis.

For current news of the California wine scene, there are several excellent weekly news columns, among them: Bob Thompson's "Living Wine" in the *San Francisco Examiner*, Henry Rubin's "The Winemaster" in the *San Francisco Chronicle* and Nathan Chroman's column in the *Los Angeles Times*. There are interesting wine columns in several magazines, of which Bob Thompson's in *San Francisco* magazine and Gerald Asher's "Wine Journal" in *Gourmet* magazine are among the finest.

There are several fine magazines devoted primarily to wine, among them *Wine World, Vintage, Bon Appétit,* and, from England, the *Journal of the International Wine and Food Society* (formerly *Food and Wine*). *Wine Magazine* is not being published at the moment. The trade magazine, *Wines and Vines*, often has articles which are of interest to the consumer.

The wine newsletters and buyers' guides can be very useful, provided that they are not taken too seriously. These guides can often direct a discriminating buyer to wines which he might enjoy very much, particularly the finer wines of limited quantity which do not remain on the market for very long. Of course, no one can possibly dictate what wines one will actually enjoy. It is impossible to make definitive, infallible judgments which will be valid for all palates. I have enjoyed many wines which have been passed over or have been given disparaging reviews in these guides. It is advisable to get a second opinion on the wines from your wine merchant.

I have found the following wine guides particularly helpful. The list does not include some other less practical and less thorough guides which many people will enjoy reading for news and anecdotes about wine.

Connoisseur's Guide to California Wine
P.O. Box 11120
San Francisco, California 94101

International Wine Letter and Digest
111 New Montgomery Street
San Francisco, California 94105

Robert Finigan's Private Guide to Wines
100 Bush Street
San Francisco, California 94104

Robert Lawrence Balzer's Private Guide to Food and Wine
933 Costillo Street
Santa Barbara, California 93101

The Wineries

Napa County Wineries

CALISTOGA

Carneros Creek Winery*
1285 Dealy Lane
(707) 226–3279

Chateau Montelena**
1429 Tubbs Lane
(707) 942–5105

Clos du Val**
5584 Silverado Trail
(707) 224–6378

Cuvaison
4500 Silverado Trail North
(707) 942–6100

J. Mathews Napa Valley Winery
1711 Main Street
(707) 224–3222

Diamond Creek Vineyards**
1500 Diamond Mountain Road
(415) 931–0293

Mayacamas Vineyards*
1155 Lokoya Road
(707) 224–4030

Hanns Kornell Champagne
Cellars
1091 Larkmead Lane
(707) 963–2334

Moët-Hennessy**
1743 Mt. Veeder Road
(707) 224–2022

Schramsberg Vineyards*
Schramsberg Road
(707) 942–4558

Mt. Veeder Winery*
1999 Mt. Veeder Road
(707) 224–4039

Sterling Vineyards
1111 Dunaweal Lane
(707) 942–5151

Stag's Leap Wine Cellars*
5766 Silverado Trail
(707) 255–4284

Stonegate
1183 Dunaweal Lane
(707) 942–6500

Trefethen Vineyards**
1160 Oak Knoll Avenue
(707) 255–7703

*by appointment only
**not open to the public

Veedercrest Vineyards**
2203 Mt. Veeder Road
(415) 849–3303

OAKVILLE

Robert Mondavi Winery
7801 Highway 29
(707) 963–7156

Oakville Vineyards
7840 Highway 29
(707) 944–2457

Villa Mt. Eden**
Mt. Eden Ranch
(707) 944–2045

RUTHERFORD

Beaulieu Vineyards
1960 Highway 29
(707) 963–3671

Inglenook Vineyards
Highway 29
(707) 963–7182

Souverain Cellars
Souverain Road and Silverado
Trail
(707) 963–2759

ST. HELENA

Beringer Winery
2000 Main Street
(707) 963–7115

Burgess Cellars
1108 Deer Park Road
(707) 963–4766

Caymus Vineyards*
8700 Conn Creek Road
(707) 963–4204

Chappellet Vineyards*
1581 Sage Canyon Road
(707) 963–7136

Chateau Chevalier*
3101 Spring Mountain Road
(707) 963–2342

Christian Brothers Winery
2555 North Main Street
(707) 963–2719

Conradi Vineyards*
3650 Spring Mountain Road
(707) 963–7511

Franciscan Vineyards
1179 Galleron Road
(707) 963–3886

Freemark Abbey Winery
3022 St. Helena Highway
(707) 963–7106

Heitz Wine Cellars
500 St. Helena Highway
(707) 963–3542

Charles Krug Winery
Highway 29
(707) 963–2761

Louis Martini Winery
Highway 29
(707) 963–2736

Nichelini Vineyards
Highway 128
(707) 963–3357

Joseph Phelps Vineyards*
200 Taplin Road
(707) 963–2745

Pope Valley Winery
6613 Pope Valley Road
(707) 963–2192

Spring Mountain Vineyards*
2805 Spring Mountain Road
(707) 963–4341

Stony Hill Vineyard*
3331 North St. Helena Highway
(707) 963–2636

Sutter Home Winery
277 St. Helena Highway
(707) 963–3104

Yverdon Vineyards**
3728 Spring Mountain Road
(707) 963–3266

Chateau St. Jean
8555 Sonoma Highway
(707) 833–4134

YOUNTVILLE

Stag's Leap Winery**
Stag's Leap Ranch
(707) 944–2792

SONOMA

Buena Vista Winery
P.O. Box 500, Old Winery Road
(707) 938–8504

Sonoma County Wineries

Hacienda Wine Cellars
1000 Vineyard Lane
(707) 938–2244

GLEN ELLEN

Grand Cru Vineyards*
1 Vintage Lane
(707) 996–8100

Hanzell Vineyards*
18596 Lomita Avenue
(707) 996–3860

Valley of the Moon Winery
777 Madrone Road
(707) 996–6941

Sebastiani Vineyards
389 Fourth Street
(707) 938–5532

KENWOOD

Kenwood Vineyards
P.O. Box 447
(707) 833–5891

Z-D Wines*
P.O. Box 900, 20735 Burndale
Road

ASTI

Italian Swiss Colony
P.O. Box 1
(707) 894–2541

CLOVERDALE

Bandiera Wines
155 Cherry Creek Road
(707) 894–5887

Rege Wine Company
26885 Redwood Highway
(415) 891–1161

FORESTVILLE

Russian River Vineyards
5700 Gravenstein Highway
North
(707) 887–2243

Joseph Swan Vineyards*
2916 Laguna Road
(707) 546–7711

GEYSERVILLE

Geyser Peak Winery
Redwood Highway North
(707) 433–6585

Nervo Winery
19585 Redwood Highway South
(707) 857–9902

J. Pedroncelli Winery
1220 Canyon Road
(707) 857–3619

Souverain of Alexander Valley
19058 Redwood Highway South
(707) 857–3789

Trentadue Winery
19170 Redwood Highway South
(707) 433–3104

GUERNEVILLE

Korbel Winery
Korbel Station
(707) 887–2294

HEALDSBURG

Cambiaso Winery
1141 Grant Avenue
(707) 433–1937

Dry Creek Vineyard
3770 Lambert Bridge Road
(707) 433–1000

L. Foppiano Vineyards
12707 Old Redwood
Highway
(707) 433–1937

Simi Winery
P.O. Box 946
(707) 433–4276

SANTA ROSA

Martini & Prati Wines, Inc.
2191 Laguna Road
(707) 823–2404

WINDSOR

Sonoma Vineyards
P.O. Box 57, Old Redwood
Highway
(707) 433–5545

Mendocino County Wineries

PHILO

Edmeades Vineyards
5500 Highway 128
(707) 895–3232

Husch Vineyards*
P.O. Box 144

REDWOOD VALLEY

Fetzer Vineyards
1150 Bel Arbres Road
(707) 485–8671

Weibel Champagne Vineyards
7051 North State Street
(707) 485–0321

UKIAH

Cresta Blanca
539-H North State Street
(707) 462-0565

Parducci Wine Cellars
501 Parducci Road
(707) 462-3828

Contra Costa/ Solano Wineries

FAIRFIELD

Cadenasso Winery
P.O. Box 22
(707) 425-5845

MARTINEZ

J. E. Digardi Winery
3785 Pacheco Blvd.
(415) 228-2638

Conrad Viano Winery
150 Morello Road
(415) 228-2638

SUISUN CITY

Wooden Valley Winery
Route 1, P.O. Box 124
(707) 425-3962

Lodi District Wineries

ACAMPO

Barengo Cellars
P.O. Box A, Acampo Road
(209) 369-2746

LOCKEFORD

Lockeford Winery
Locke Road
(209) 727-5541

LODI

Coloma Cellars
22291 N. DeVries Road
(209) 368-7822

East-Side Winery
(Royal Host)
6100 E. Highway 12
(209) 369–4768

Winemasters' Guild
One Winemasters' Way
(209) 368–5151

Sierra Foothills Wineries

EL DORADO COUNTY

Coloma Cellars
P.O. Box 270, Coloma
(916) 622–2275

Gold Hill Winery
P.O. Box 267, Coloma
(916) 622–1712

AMADOR COUNTY

Amador Winery
P.O. Box 246, Amador City
(209) 267–5320

D'Agostini Winery
Route 2, Box 19, Plymouth
(209) 245–6612

Monteviña*
Route 2, Box 30A, Plymouth
(209) 245–3176

TUOLUMNE COUNTY

Butler Winery
Route 3, Box 357, Sonora
(209) 586–4384

Columbia Cellars
P.O. Box 629, Columbia
(209) 984–3727

Santa Clara Valley Wineries

CUPERTINO

Ridge Vineyards*
17100 Monte Bello Road
(408) 867–3233

GILROY

Bertero Winery
3920 Hecker Pass Highway
(408) 842–3032

Bonesio Winery
11550 Watsonville Road
(408) 842–2601

Conrotto Winery
1690 Hecker Pass Highway
(408) 842–3053

Fortino Winery
4525 Hecker Pass Highway
(408) 842–3305

Thomas Kruse
4390 Hecker Pass Highway
(408) 842–7016

Live Oaks Winery
3875 Hecker Pass Highway
(408) 842–2401

Rapazzini's Los Altos Winery
P.O. Box 247
(408) 842–5649

LOS GATOS

Almaden Vineyards
Blossom Hill Road
(408) 269–1312

David Bruce*
21439 Bear Creek Road
(408) 354–4214

Novitiate of Los Gatos
P.O. Box 128 (College Avenue)
(408) 354–6471

MORGAN HILL

Filice Winery
1110 San Pedro Avenue
(408) 779–2415

E. Guglielmo Winery
East Main Avenue
(408) 779–3064

Pedrizetti Winery
San Pedro Avenue
(408) 779–3710

Richert & Sons, Inc.
1120 North El Camino Real
(408) 779–3919

MOUNTAIN VIEW

Gemello Winery
2003 El Camino Real
(415) 948–7723

PORTOLA VALLEY

Nepenthe Cellars*
216 Corte Madera Road

SAN JOSE

Mirassou Vineyards
Route 3, Box 344,
Aborn Road
(408) 274–4000

SAN MARTIN

San Martin Vineyards
P.O. Box 53
(408) 683–2672

SARATOGA

Mt. Eden Vineyards*
22000 Mt. Eden Road
(408) 867–5783

Paul Masson Vineyards
13150 Saratoga Avenue
(408) 257–7800

WOODSIDE

Sherrill Cellars*
P.O. Box 4155
(415) 851–1932

Woodside Winery*
340 Kings Mountain Road
(415) 851–7475

Alameda County Wineries

ALBANY

Davis Bynum Winery
614 San Pablo Avenue
(415) 526–1366

BERKELEY

Oak Barrel Winery
1201 University Avenue
(415) 849–0400

LIVERMORE

Concannon Vineyard
4590 Tesla Road
(415) 447–3760

Wente Brothers
5565 Tesla Road
(415) 447–3603

MISSION SAN JOSE

Weibel Champagne
Vineyards
1250 Stanford Avenue
(415) 656–9914

PLEASANTON

Ruby Hill Vineyard
1188 Vineyard Avenue
(415) 846–2004

Villa Armando
553 St. John Street
(415) 846–5488

Santa Cruz/ Monterey District Wineries

SANTA CRUZ COUNTY

Bargetto's Santa Cruz Winery
3535 North Main Street, Soquel
(408) 475–2258

Locatelli Winery*
P.O. Box 106, Boulder Creek
(408) 338–6115

Nicasio Vineyards
14300 Nicasio Way, Soquel
(408) 423–1073

Roudon-Smith Vineyards
513 Mt. View Road, Santa Cruz
(408) 292–5884

MONTEREY COUNTY

Chalone Vineyard*
P.O. Box 855, Soledad
655 Sutter Street, San Francisco
(415) 441–8975

Monterey Peninsula Winery
299 Monterey/Salinas Highway,
Monterey
(408) 372–4949

Monterey Vineyards Inc.
P.O. Box 650, Gonzales
(408) 675–2326
600 Montgomery St.,
San Francisco
(415) 986–2650

San Luis Obispo District Wineries

PASO ROBLES

Hoffman Mountain Ranch
Vineyards
P.O. Box 232 (24th Street)
(805) 238–4945

TEMPLETON

Pesenti Winery
Route 1, Box 169
(Vineyard Drive)
(805) 434–1030

Rotta Winery
Route 1, Box 168
(Vineyard Drive)
(805) 434–1389

York Mountain Winery
Route 1, Box 191
(York Mountain Road)
(805) 238–3925

The Central Valley Wineries

BUTTE COUNTY

Butte Creek Vineyards
$2623\frac{1}{2}$ Esplanada, Chico
(916) 345–3075

SACRAMENTO COUNTY

Corti Brothers
5760 Freeport Blvd., Sacramento
(916) 391–0300

James Frasinetti & Sons
P.O. Box 28213, Sacramento
(916) 383–2444

Gibson Wine Company
P.O. Drawer E, Elk Grove
(916) 685–9594

Harbor Winery*
610 Harbor Blvd.,
West Sacramento

SAN JOAQUIN COUNTY

Bella Napoli Winery
21128 South Austin Road,
Manteca
(209) 599–3835

Cadlolo Winery
1124 California Street,
Escalon
(209) 838–2457

Delicato Winery
12001 South Highway 99,
Manteca
(209) 823–5616

Franzia Brothers Winery
P.O. Box 697, Ripon
(209) 599–4251

STANISLAUS COUNTY

E. & J. Gallo**
P.O. Box 1130, Modesto
(209) 521–3111

Pirrone Wine Cellars
P.O. Box 15, Salida
(209) 545–0704

MADERA COUNTY

Bisceglia Brothers Wine
Company
25427 Avenue 13, Madera
(209) 673–3594

Ficklin Vineyards*
30246 Avenue $7\frac{1}{2}$, Madera
(209) 674–4598

FRESNO COUNTY

Del Rey Winery
5427 East Central Ave., Fresno
(209) 264–2901

Farnesi Winery
2426 Almond Ave., Sanger
(209) 875–3004

Golden State Winery*
2234 West Dakota Ave.,
Fresno
(209) 229–0249

Landis Vineyard*
2068 East Clayton Ave.,
Fresno
(209) 264–0304

A. Nonini Winery
2640 North Dickenson Ave.,
Fresno
(209) 264–7857

Roma Winery
3223 East Church Ave.,
Fresno
(209) 485–3080

Nicholas G. Verry, Inc.
400 First Street, Parlier
(209) 646–2785

TULARE COUNTY

California Growers Winery
P.O. Box 38, Cutler
(209) 528–3033

Robert Setrakian Vineyards**
P.O. Box 21, Yettem
(415) 398–1121

KERN COUNTY

California Wine Association*
P.O. Box 818, Delano
(805) 792–3162
851 Burlway Rd., Box 4067,
Burlingame
(415) 342–4374

Giumarra Vineyards
Highway 466, P.O. Bin 1969,
Edison
(805) 366–7251

M. Lamont
(Bear Mountain Winery)
P.O. Box 566, Lamont
(805) 845–2231

CUCAMONGA DISTRICT

Aggazzotti Winery
11929 Foothill Boulevard,
Cucamonga
(714) 987-1657

Brookside Winery
9900 A Street, Guasti
(714) 983-2787

Callaway Vineyard
and Winery
Box 257, Temecula
(714) 656-5008

Louis Cherpin Winery
15567 Valley Boulevard,
Fontana
(714) 822-4103

Ferrara Winery
1120 West 15th Avenue,
Escondido
(714) 745-7632

J. Filippi Vintage Co.
Box 2, Mira Loma
(714) 984-4514

Galleano Winery
4231 Wineville Avenue,
Mira Loma
(714) 685-5376

Llords and Elwood Winery
315 South Beverly Drive,
Beverly Hills
(213) 553-2368

Opici Winery
10150 Highland Avenue,
Alta Loma
(714) 987-2710

San Antonio Winery
737 Lamar Street,
Los Angeles
(213) 223-1401

Santa Barbara Winery
202 Anacapa Street,
Santa Barbara
(805) 966-5012

Thomas Vineyards
8916 Foothill Boulevard,
Cucamonga
(714) 987-1612

Index

Date Due			